T0114990

HEART-SHAPED ROCKS

ROCKS

A PATH TO HAPPINESS

LEE ANN PERRY

BALBOA.
PRESS

A DIVISION OF HAY HOUSE

Balboa Press books may be ordered through booksellers or by contacting:

Balboa Press
A Division of Hay House
1663 Liberty Drive
Bloomington, IN 47403
www.balboapress.com
1 (877) 407-4847

Because of the dynamic nature of the Internet, any web addresses or links contained in this book may have changed since publication and may no longer be valid. The views expressed in this work are solely those of the author and do not necessarily reflect the views of the publisher, and the publisher hereby disclaims any responsibility for them.

The author of this book does not dispense medical advice or prescribe the use of any technique as a form of treatment for physical, emotional, or medical problems without the advice of a physician, either directly or indirectly. The intent of the author is only to offer information of a general nature to help you in your quest for emotional and spiritual well-being. In the event you use any of the information in this book for yourself, which is your constitutional right, the author and the publisher assume no responsibility for your actions.

Any people depicted in stock imagery provided by Thinkstock are models, and such images are being used for illustrative purposes only. Certain stock imagery © Thinkstock.

Printed in the United States of America.

ISBN: 978-1-4525-8524-6 (sc)
ISBN: 978-1-4525-8526-0 (hc)
ISBN: 978-1-4525-8525-3 (e)

Library of Congress Control Number: 2013919271

Balboa Press rev. date: 11/07/2013

With heartfelt thanks to
Pamela Lee,
Editor extraordinaire.

Contents

1. Heart-Shaped Rocks 1
2. My Resources 4
3. Philosophical Evolution 6
4. Meeting Seth 9
5. Wedding Night 11
6. Co-Dependence 14
7. Significance 16
8. Spring Lake Five 20
9. Blake 24
10. Following My Passion 33
11. Luck & Softball 36
12. Law of Attraction 39
13. First Night 42
14. Choosing Happiness 46
15. Buried Wisdom 49
16. Depression 51
17. Counseling a Friend 54
18. No Obstacles 58
19. Justification 61
20. Re-Lifting my Mood 67
21. Prismatic Light 72
22. Meditation 74
23. Swimming in Vermont 77
24. Becoming Loving 81

25. Raindrops...83

26. College Dream 85

27. Sailing 89

28. Pleasing Others...93

29. Fairy Tales...97

30. Walking and Venting 101

31. Anger and Judgment..103

32. Beyond Fear of Negativity...................................107

33. Marriage, Worthiness, and Loving 109

34. Sea Chanties...112

35. Weez 114

36. Decisiveness 119

37. Accountability...123

38. Enlightenment and Ree 125

39. Kripalu 129

40. Practices...134

41. Dreams...137

42. Dating 144

43. Valentine's Day...145

44. Spring Break...150

45. Morning Bike Ride 152

46. Culmination..154

47. Self-Awareness...155

48. Allowing..158

49. Communion 160

50. Expansive Love..162

About the Author...165

1

Heart-Shaped Rocks

Last summer I started collecting heart-shaped rocks. Actually, I already had several, but they seem to have just appeared in my landscape. Walking out in the yard, I sometimes noticed rocks that had been revealed by a hard rain, or when Buddy raked up dirt in a seemingly futile attempt to cover his poop. It was Ree, my longtime guru-friend, who got me interested in collecting rocks. She referred to it as "hunting" them to add a sense of mischief, pretending they were elusive. Once I watched her struggling to extricate a small boulder from a muddy riverbank beside the path we were walking along. When the boulder slipped from her grasp and tumbled down the hill, in her *Wind in the Willows* accent she declared, "You see how they are; they try to get away." I accompanied her on a couple quests, and it wasn't long before I got caught up in the excitement of the hunt. Besides, I enjoyed believing that all things have consciousness.

Ree and I were walking along a streambed a while back. She was staring down at the rocks, looking for one with a specific configuration. Since she had been hunting for many years, her garden needed only embellishment, whereas mine was comparatively devoid of rocks. I was watching the sunlight dancing through the water, and spotted a smallish stone which, with vivid imagination, could be considered fish-shaped. I brought it to Ree's attention. She regarded it neutrally, then suggested I think about a shape I would delight in finding. After that I started looking for hearts.

Even the idea of looking for symbols of love appealed to me. When Rockefeller—or somebody who had amassed an enormous fortune—was asked how he came to have so much money, he replied, "I look for it." Well then, I would seek my fortune in hearts. Heart-shaped leaves, heart-shaped clouds . . . I started humming "Love is in the Air," as my mind filled with a stream of connected images on the theme.

Love is the domain of my alignment. Actually, I believe it is the foundation of all that is good. When things are right in my world, I feel in the flow of love. And when things are not right, I assume "Love is the answer"—not just *my* answer, an integral part of the natural order. Love forms the boundaries of my comfort zone. Out of love is out of well-being. I have always recognized that the two were connected, but I never really studied the anatomy of my well-being—not until recently, when events transpired that rocked my world.

It took a lot to rock my world because I believed adversity could be turned into opportunity. That attitude serves me well in my job counseling high school kids. Fears of rejection or failure, which stem from feeling vulnerable, crop up a lot in that world. When kids feel powerless, I help them shift their perspectives, get them to focus forward, and rekindle their sense of possibility. Some kids have a remarkable ability to transcend adversity while others linger around hopelessness and depression. I was determined to show up on the resilient end of the spectrum.

Although I suffered the emotional undertow of a divorce, I was able to maneuver out of depression, to reclaim optimism. In fact, people around me began asking how I got into such a good space. The answer came through an evolution of perception about my well-being. I thought about it a lot, I talked about it a lot, and gradually I came to view my experience from a state of appreciation.

⇥ 2 ⇤

My Resources

When I first acknowledged that my marriage was over, I kept asking the question, "How on earth did this go down in *my* life? How could someone as accommodating and positive as I be getting divorced?" After all, I believed I was on a path of enlightenment and that I influenced my circumstances. I knew there had been a lot wrong in our relationship, but I clung to the hope that I could turn things around. Apparently, I had fantasized that we were drifting toward the sunset. Perhaps I should have been steering? I thought that if I wrote down my story, then read it and pictured it as a play, I could consider the experience objectively.

So I began to write, and it turned into a process of self-discovery, even surprise. It did not escape my notice that the parts that gave me the most trouble were the ones in which I saw myself as a victim and felt justified. Fortunately, that agenda found its nemesis in something like a moral imperative: I was committed to taking an enlightened view of it all. Being loving was the only acceptable course for me.

I had a lot of resources to call on for support and insight. Daily I walked along the lake to access inner guidance; I met with or called Ree and gained deeper insights from her channeling. She held me accountable to my stated intention, to find the gift in this apparent adversity. It was always easier to find a broader perspective at the ocean where I so easily attuned to my expanded sense of who-I-really-am.

At the Jersey shore, I could connect with another astute sounding board, Larry. He has been my friend ever since my Washington Crossing days when I shared a house (we called it "Fort Apache") with Ree and Weez—a defining chapter of my life.

When the impulse strikes, I drive down to the shore. I stand alone at the water's edge until I am sated with salt air and spray, feeling one with all that is. Then I like to sit and talk with Larry on his porch overlooking the ocean. I had told him what I was up to, and he was supportive with ideas to keep my writing flowing. Having written several books himself, he is abundantly familiar with the introspection process. He got it when I told him that I kept coming up with different starting points for my story, and suggested that I consider writing about my philosophical evolution rather than giving a chronological accounting of events. I was curious to see where focusing on my philosophical evolution might lead.

✣ 3 ✣

Philosophical Evolution

My mind was teeming with ideas as I drove home; I could hardly wait to get my journal open. No sooner did I start to organize my thoughts than it occurred to me that I made no distinction between my philosophical evolution and my spiritual evolution, and I knew precisely the event to begin writing about.

There was a turning point in the evolution of my spirituality that took place on a beautiful spring afternoon when I was a teenager, watching a baseball game. My boyfriend, Denny, was warming up to pitch. I was sitting in the bleachers, soaking up sunshine, when I tuned in to a conversation behind me. I turned around to be part of it and recognized one of the speakers. John was talking about Edgar Cayce, and I found what he was saying so riveting that I could barely pay attention to the game. Cayce wrote that God is like a library in which we are all books. My mind reeled as I reconsidered my connection to God. Sister Margaret, my Sunday school nun, had said, "You never have to feel alone; you can talk to God at any time," and I took that on faith. In fact, I had often had conversations with God, but that was the first time I had considered myself a *part* of God.

John went on about akashic records and God-energy. I was blown away by what he was saying. We can each tap into that energy. I remember how wonderful I felt, warm sunlight beaming on me, my mind exploding with possibilities; I wanted to fly off the bleachers and go buy the book so that I could read it myself. For the first time, I entertained the notion that I had a part in my destiny.

The bookstore shelved Edgar Cayce's *Akashic Records— Book of Life*, in the Spiritual section. That became one of my favorite destinations. I gravitated toward themes of love, or maybe I was just reading love into everything. By the time I got to college, I was seeing how love tied in to all situations, how love was the solution to all problems. Sure enough, my World Religions course confirmed what I already believed: love is humanity's common language. And my heart was fluent in it.

Larry shares my enthusiasm for the Spiritual and Self-Help sections of bookstores, and has read and absorbed so much that he could generate a reference guide for those genres. He sees where various concepts overlap and which authors present truly novel perspectives. He puts Napoleon Hill in that category.

I often followed Larry's reading recommendations, but I was turned off by the title *Think and Grow Rich*; it just seemed so . . . mercenary. Then one day I was cruising through Barnes and Noble when a copy of that book jumped out at me. Intrigued, I opened it at random to "Every adversity, every failure and every heartache carries with it the seed of an equivalent or a greater benefit." Twenty minutes later, I was still reading. Finally, I purchased the book and took it to the café in the back of the store, where I could sit and contemplate Hill's assertion, "Through the faculty of creative imagination, the finite mind of man has direct communication with Infinite Intelligence."

A lot of what I read reinforced ideas that I had been considering and discussing with the gang at Fort Apache, but "tapping the source of inspiration" was new. Unfortunately, it was time to go, so my curiosity would have to wait until I found another unclaimed block of time.

In the magical way that one thought leads to another, I recalled studying different counseling theories in graduate school. I had two favorites: Self-Actualization Theory, and Rational Emotive Therapy, and I could hardly wait to apply them in a teaching situation.

The language Carl Rogers used in his Self-Actualization Theory was inspirational. He wrote of an "inborn drive to grow and develop to our highest level of human beingness." Those words thrilled me. That was the potential I wanted express and to inspire others with. Rogers believed that all people were inherently good and creative, but became destructive if their environment did not support them. I agreed wholeheartedly.

Albert Ellis' assertion that we have a choice regarding how we react to our experiences validated my belief that I could hold to a loving space regardless of my situation. It also provided me with a powerful tool to help kids separate what they considered obligatory reactions ("should . . . , ought to . . . ," and "must . . ." directives) from their perceived experiences, and choose responses that better served them. I loved it.

The counseling theories I gravitated to became like spiritual theories for me. Part of my path of enlightenment, they melded with my craving to know all the facets of love. What makes some people light-hearted. How could I lighten people's hearts?

I remembered the almost uncontainable excitement I had felt, driving in to work the morning after a theory class, bursting with eagerness to share my enthusiasm with my colleague, Seth, anticipating the combustion that always transpired during our conversations. Then I found myself examining what had made me fall for Seth in the first place.

⇥ 4 ⇤

Meeting Seth

When I met Seth, my personal/career goals were becoming clearer. I wanted to be an inspiring teacher. I knew I was already a very good teacher, and I knew I could be even better. I wanted to be one who exudes unconditional love, who is non-judgmental regardless of kids' choices. My situation was perfect. I was starting a new job at Highpoint School. The kids who showed up there had serious emotional issues; it was not a stretch to say they were tough kids to teach—just the challenge I was looking for. I was surrounded by like-minded, supportive co-workers, and encouraged by a thoroughly charismatic leader, Seth.

Seth was fresh from the inner city Philadelphia alternative school system. He had just been appointed principal of Highpoint, and he was fired up to make a difference. His enthusiasm was contagious. Seth so firmly believed he could turn the kids around and transform their lives, he got the whole teaching staff to buy into his vision. The staff and kids all stretched to reach his high standards. Part of Seth's success with the kids was getting them to want to comply. He set up systems whereby kids could earn the privilege of doing something fun like playing hoops with him. And he'd be out there on the court to tempt them and make playing worth earning.

Lee Ann Perry

As principal, Seth was the disciplinarian. Crisis management was an art in that school expressly established for challenging behavior, and Seth had a real talent for reaching the kids. His goal was to get them to believe they could make their lives better, govern their impulses, and make good choices. He enrolled them in recognizing the consequences of their actions and resolving the conflicts they found themselves in. Seth knew (and probably they knew, too) that if a kid did not make it there, the next stop was an institutional placement. Seth did everything in his power, physically and emotionally, to convince the kids to work with him there in that situation. If not for his strong leadership and established support network, a lot of those kids would have been moved out, "downgraded." Seth never gave up on a kid, and he never backed down from a position. The kids learned that he could out wait them, out calm them, and out reason them in any confrontation. The power of Seth's authority and his tenacity worked with the kids at Highpoint. That same unyielding stance later played out as a stalemate in our relationship.

So that was it. What had drawn me to Seth—and upturned my world—had been his inspiration, and the exhilaration of shared passion, our common burning desire to uplift kids. To this day, I can get into that zone when Seth and I talk about education—that and talk about our kids. On other topics . . . not so much, but conversation about inspiring kids is always good common ground. It was a big part of the chemistry that brought us together.

Knowing how committed Seth could be, and how well we worked together, I envisioned ours would be a relationship of co-creation. That was what I was going for—and thought I was getting—when I said, "I do." Leading up to the ceremony, our relationship had been brimming with romance and play. Then we got married.

⊰ 5 ⊱

Wedding Night

In hindsight, it seems as though the period before we were married was the honeymoon. Things changed abruptly right after the wedding. Actually, things changed abruptly *during* the wedding when I almost bit off Seth's thumb. I can explain.

Our wedding cake was created from Hazelnut Torte, one of my favorite desserts. Ever since we tasted the caterer's sample, I was eager to devour more. However, when dessert time came, I realized that my cake consumption would be a public display; in front of all our guests, I would reveal a personal flaw: I could not bite cleanly through things. Some of my teeth are misaligned. I probably should have had braces. Anyway, it has been a lifelong source of insecurity, not being able to sever food evenly; I always end up kind of shredding it. So, not wanting to make a spectacle of my ceremonial "first bite of sweetness," and determined not to wimp out as I began my new life, I was decisive in my approach, and chomped down hard on what I perceived to be a hazelnut in the proffered slice of wedding cake. To ensure the success of my endeavor, I even added a few quick slashing moves with my faulty incisors. All the subsequent pictures showed my husband with a napkin tourniquet over his bloody paw.

Aside from that, the wedding was wonderful. We were outside on a gorgeous Sunday afternoon at a quaint inn in the country. I was distracted from listening to the ceremonial words by the enchanting sounds of the waterfall behind us.

We had booked the inn's wedding suite for that night, and I was anticipating blowing Seth's mind—at the very least. We went to our room and shed our formal clothes. I put on the little something daring; I could hardly wait to surprise Seth. After my costume change, I emerged from the bathroom eager to enact my transformation from blushing bride to brazen seductress, determined to push past any emotional barriers (ignoring the hazelnut episode), and take the initiative for the first time. It had been so much fun rehearsing for this moment in front of a mirror with Weez and Ree, cracking up over their hysterical charades— each of us trying to outdo the others' performances— demonstrating how I would saunter to the nuptial bed jutting my voluptuous breasts, wearing my lace-trimmed teddy with a quick-release one-snap crotch. I was ready.

Alas, Seth was not. I was too deflated to take in what he said—something about not expecting that we would have sex just because we were married. In my insecurity, I wondered if my approach had been a turn-off. Or was he afraid of my teeth? Seth's reaction was so far from what I had been expecting, I had no idea what to say, and I certainly did not want to have a confrontation on our wedding night. To begin with, confrontation was way out of my comfort zone. I considered that maybe he just didn't feel up to performing because he was so tired; admittedly, it had been a long emotional day. But, had his tone actually been dismissive, or was that my insecurity again?

At the reception, Seth's college friends had made such a big deal over the fact that Seth had actually "gone through with it." I had smiled brightly as they shared their astonishment, "We never thought we'd see the day . . . So you're the one than finally pinned him down." In the shadow cast by Seth's rejection however, their comments plagued me. I had definitely gotten Seth's attachment—my ring was evidence—but would I be able to keep it?

The thought that Seth did not find me desirable was simply unacceptable. I was desperate for assurance that things were fine between us. My intuition was on Red Alert, but I overrode it with hopeful excuses, and convinced myself that I was okay with it all. It was the beginning of a long period of doubt and denial.

As I watched my husband fall asleep, I sat there trying to work out a plausible story to justify his behavior. I tried to recount some of the fun moments of the day, but I just couldn't get comfortable because the neglected teddy was giving me a wedgie. Eventually I drifted off with a romantic melody repeating in my mind. I figured with a start like that things could only get better.

⊰ 6 ⊱

Co-Dependence

Dispassionately reflecting on what I had written, I had stepped off a path of enlightenment—on this issue at least—and it was glaringly apparent that I had been preoccupied with how I came off in Seth's assessment. Undeniable co-dependence. Not in the classical textbook sense, mine wasn't a pathological addictive dependence. My co-dependence fell into one of the definitions from *Co-Dependents Anonymous* "placing a lower priority on one's own needs, while being excessively preoccupied with the needs of others." It reminded me of something Ree used to quote to me when I took the part of victim of my situation: "On top of every 'doormat' is a person desperate to get off."

Throughout our relationship I was aware of Seth's unwillingness to curtail his freedom, but I was determined to maintain his attachment. In my craving for his approval, I downplayed any evidence of his rejection, tweaking it to be motivation for my growth, and I was proud of my psychological spin. I believed my attitude represented an inclination for self-improvement. I even convinced myself that it was a mutual goal. I transmuted my feelings of inadequacy to my desire for enlightenment.

I was fond of the expression "Happiness comes from within;" I even bought into it intellectually, but I did not really live it when it came to Seth. Back then, my idea of being happy was seeing Seth happy with me. Predictably, the more I sought his reassurance, the more he distanced himself. Our relationship proceeded in a downward spiral as I acted from my co-dependent mindset.

Our wedding night marked the beginning of an era of selective focus on my part. I deliberately disregarded what I sensed as disturbing, and distracted myself with thoughts of positive things: "Tomorrow we will be on our way to Nova Scotia. I'll be in my perfect environment with the man I love. I'm tired too; we can both use a night's sleep." My selective attention was half of an excellent formula for feeling good. But the other half is based in self-assuredness—and mine was not firmly anchored around Seth.

Something else jumped out at me as I wrote. Before this scrutiny, I had maintained that what was lacking was honest, open communication. Now I get that my communication would have been powerful only if it had been delivered with unfiltered confidence. That was not where I was then. The real problem was my own fear of rejection. While it was perfectly reasonable that I did not want to spoil a beautiful occasion with confrontation, my reluctance to communicate was an indicator of a deeper insecurity about our relationship: I subconsciously doubted it could survive full disclosure.

⚜ 7 ⚜

Significance

When I told Larry about looking for the disconnect between my core beliefs and my experience, he came back with, "You keep trying to understand how you ended up in a dysfunctional relationship." I knew what he was going to say next. Sure enough, he quoted Werner Erhard, "Understanding is the booby prize." I should have asked what the real prize was. Appreciation? Acceptance? Experience? Probably something along those lines. But right then, I was going for understanding.

Actually, no. I wasn't going for understanding so I could intellectualize the experience *instead* of feeling it. I was looking for an alternative perspective, something unfamiliar, a new tool. I was used to just feeling my way through situations, tuning in to my heart chakra. However, I thought I had been following my heart, yet I had arrived at an unwanted outcome—irrefutable evidence that something was off in my approach. Either some principle or belief was present that was not serving me, or something was missing that was necessary for my success. In either case I was motivated to examine my process of perception; I felt inclined to do my exploring from a more mental realm.

Casper was sprawled out on the window seat, drenched in sunlight. I imagined him happy as a cat could be—napping. It struck me that I had been following my own version of cat wisdom: enjoy what is there to be enjoyed; move off whatever is not pleasing. No analysis. Except the cat had good results. He got fed, stroked, and appreciated without any real effort on his part. What wasn't I getting about this?

Sometimes writing my story was like pushing a rope— there was no making it go straight. It frustrated me because I was determined to make sense of it all. Larry kept hinting that it did not necessarily make sense. But I needed it to. Once, after I had recounted an episode to him which I considered to be fraught with relevance, he had the audacity to chuckle. I protested, reemphasizing the significant elements. Tactfully, he dismissed any significance as my interpretation only, and segued into a workshop experience.

Larry was saying that all experience is arrived at through interpretation. I was moving the idea around in my mind to see whether I agreed with him or not, then tuned back in at the word "construct." What if he was right, that I had *constructed* the significance of my story? My mind wandered.

Besides having provided Larry with lots of wonderful insights, Werner Erhard had been instrumental in connecting him with his bride-to-be. Weez had just finished the EST Training the weekend before they met. She was high on life, swaying to the jazz playing at a favorite hangout in New Hope, and fell into conversation, sharing her enthusiasm with some of the regulars. At some point in her fumbled attempts to explain the source of her newfound joy, Larry, who had been watching her and listening, stepped into the conversation, and deftly turned it to her advantage. He won the point and the heart of the girl in the process.

Just from hanging around them, I have come to adopt several of their Training aphorisms as my own. One that I have used a lot in my counseling is, "It is easier to ride the horse in the direction it is going." Kids often walk out my door nodding sagely when I close with that one. With his unique blend of psychology, EST, and New Age philosophy, Larry reasserted that the only significance to my story was that which I had assigned it.

I was still processing that when I drove right past Hoffman's. Ice cream was usually the grande finale in my full shore experience. A measure of consolation, it served as the lure to ease my parting from the ocean. I had not noticed any flashing turn signals from other cars preparing to negotiate the parking lot. Still, I would have thought force of habit would have at least made me check to see if it was open. It was rare for me to drive home without a half eaten cone, upturned in a cup the way I liked it, on my dashboard within nibbling range. On the other hand, it was not ice cream weather yet—at least not standing-outside-in-flip-flops-eating-ice-cream weather. That was the weather I craved, and it was just around the corner. I didn't bother with turning around. If my life—according to Larry—had no inherent significance, ice cream was probably not the solution. I would try to figure it out on my way home.

The phrase "no inherent significance" triggered a memory of my son, Jesse, at his first experience golfing. Seth had taken Jesse to a driving range to introduce him to the game. The field was strewn with golf balls, so there wasn't an obvious target. At the far end of the field, a safe way off, a family of groundhogs was munching in oblivion. Trying to come up with a helpful objective, Seth told Jesse, "Aim for the groundhogs." Jesse lined up and took swing after swing, keenly focused on his task. After a while Seth added, "You know, Jesse, on a real golf course there won't be groundhogs," to which Jesse retorted, "Then what's the point?" whereupon the two animal-lovers burst out laughing.

Maybe I could be making a game out of this. If there is no inherent significance, what about making up some? Just at that thought I was passing a bank of daffodils. Nature's smile. My story could be a game of appreciating nature—better still, appreciating all that is.

⪥ 8 ⪤

Spring Lake Five

According to a landscape designer I once met, a gardener's calendar is based on key horticultural activities. Dates like St. Patrick's Day and Mother's Day signal the first time to mow the grass, and the last time to prune woody shrubs— or maybe it was the other way around. He rattled off a bunch of dates and corresponding horticultural activities. My ignorance of those rules explains a lot about my garden. The fact that I have a garden, despite my negligence, is a testimonial to Mother Nature.

Larry does not go by the standard calendar either; he reads people. For him, the advent of summer is not so much a date as it is an attitude. According to Larry, summer begins with the running of the Spring Lake 5. From his new home office he has an unobstructed view of the ocean. He had expected to sit at his desk there and be inspired to write. Instead, he sits at his desk overcome by the majesty of the vista. He gets absorbed in observing people on the boardwalk as they move across his sight frame. On bicycles, pushing wheelchairs or strollers, jogging, or inching along with walkers. Old, young, fit, out of shape. Singles, couples, families, sets of friends. He can't help analyzing them; he's a psychologist. Even when the window is closed and he can't hear their conversation, his mind fills in dialog. He is like a veterinarian, reliant on non-verbal communication. Anyway, Larry insists that people behave differently after the Spring Lake Five, so that is what he considers the real start of summer.

I never used to train for it physically; my race preparation was mostly mental. But since I've become a Zumba junkie, this year I'm expecting a personal best—if not my fastest, certainly my most energetic race. I feel obliged to point out that the five refers to miles, not kilometers, or as Jay (Weez and Larry's son, a precociously athletic child) put it, "five grueling miles, uphill both ways." Getting my registration in on time is a priority. I want the complimentary glass they give to the participants as much as I want the starting line atmosphere. Admittedly, each year's commemorative glass is slightly different. Nonetheless, together they match well enough to be considered a set by my standards.

The Spring Lake Five has always been scheduled for Memorial Day weekend, the time we traditionally held our extended family gathering. Weez used to proclaim the run to be the launching point for our summer fitness regime. The thundering rock music and starting gun shot made for a dramatic take-off, and Bruce Springsteen pumped up the collective adrenaline in a mega-amplification of *"Born to Run"*—ironic, because the crowd at the starting line was so packed, you practically had to jog in place for the first minute, and then incrementally increase your pace for the first quarter mile, as the crowd spread out. When the kids ran with us, they were usually more adept at working their way through the throng and finding open space sooner—at least that's how we liked to justify our race time differences. Sometimes we ran together, taking turns talking or encouraging each other. The ones who finished first cheered the subsequent ones across the finish line. After it was over we would bask out in the back yard thinking that Labor Day, when we would reconvene and debrief, was far in the distant future.

During the weekend of the race, and afterwards periodically throughout the summer, different pairs from our group would go for walks and talks along the boardwalk. Each pair had a different chemistry and a different pace. Since Larry's legs are several inches longer than mine, I have to trot a step every ten or so whenever we walk together. It is worth the syncopated scurry to have the camaraderie and conversation.

Whenever we get together it starts with, "Who's going first?" Then whichever of us is most keen starts in. One subject connects to the next like tipping dominoes branching and radiating out. We don't try to confine the conversation to a logical progression, just describe the thought stream as it unfurls. The best conversations are almost a competition between compelling ideas gathering momentum, all spoken over the noise of the surf.

Some subjects carry over past the turning point of our walk, but usually that is the time we switch roles from principally listening to principally speaking. Once, as we were just about to the turning point of our walk, I managed to succinctly wrap up a particularly complicated story. I concluded with, "Your turn," whereupon Larry violated our unspoken code; he stopped. "What's amazing about this yarn is that you managed to bring it back around. If Weez had been telling the story, it would have been very interesting, but it would not have had any cohesive point." That gave me the idea of seeing how elaborate I could make a story without losing the thread of it. I got to practice this game a lot during the time I was writing down my story.

Once I began telling Larry about different chapters I was working on, our walks took on a story-time quality. I would recount episodes, and Larry would ask clarifying questions. Sometimes we would explore the threads he pulled out right then; sometimes I would contemplate them on my own later. Afterwards, I often rewrote sections to include the new insights. Larry and I go way back. He has long been my confidante, so it is rare that I surprise him. But I surprised him with Blake.

9

Blake

Actually, I surprised myself in the sense that I had not thought about Blake for years. He sprang to mind as I was reconstructing the day that Seth and I met.

As Seth addressed the faculty that first day at Highpoint, it came to me in a torrent of awareness, that he embodied exactly what I wanted in a mate. I fell in love in that moment. The problem was, I had just gotten back from my honeymoon two weeks before.

Larry was quiet for a while. Then he said, "I guess I knew that you had been married before, but I never knew the details. It doesn't seem like a withhold; I'm just surprised it never came up."

I agreed. It was weird that I forgot—or blocked out—so much from that time. That was part of what I wanted to look at. From what I had been piecing together, I tried to recount my story of Blake.

Blake was a genuinely nice guy. He was sweet, funny, and drop-dead gorgeous without being stuck-up about it. My Aunt Jenny thought he looked so much like Elvis Presley she used to hum, *"You Ain't Nothin' But A Hound Dog"* whenever she saw him. My college roommates thought Blake was an awesome catch, and they were not subtle in their approval.

They tried to prod the two of us to intimacy by blasting suggestive songs like *"Tonight's the Night"* when he came over. But it wasn't. Blake was never pushy. He just adored me and put me on a pedestal.

It was certainly cool being courted by him. Who wouldn't want to be adored by a kind, handsome guy? I just had not experienced enough of life—at least not of independent life—to know what I wanted. I didn't even know who I was. There was something artificial in my persona, and I didn't know where to begin to root it out. Nor would I even do it if it involved being unkind. It was a stalemate. Blake was persistent, and I was not in the habit of disappointing. In the end, I was carried where the stronger current took me. Back then I did not trust my own instincts. Factoring-in what I thought others wanted was still a huge part of how I defined myself, and a lot of people thought that Blake was simply awesome.

After we graduated, Blake and I both moved back to our home towns, so we were six hours apart by car. We took turns visiting one another every other weekend or so. He drove out to see me; I took the bus out to see him. If I had not been distracted by my new life, my challenging job, my exciting new co-workers, the trip would not have felt like a burden.

Everything about my career had fallen into place as if by magic. It was a tough job market; nonetheless, I landed a teaching assistantship before I had even graduated. The principal was so impressed by my instant rapport with the students that, when the lead teacher walked off the job two weeks into it, I was asked to fill the vacancy.

Walking past the faculty room on my first day as lead teacher, I heard my colleagues taking bets on "how long this one would last." (The previous three teachers had given up after a few weeks.) Even without experience, I knew I would find a way to get through to my kids.

I stood at the front of the class, smiling, as the 12 boys, ages 15 to 18, came running into the classroom, laughing and shoving each other. I asked them to find seats, and to my relief, they all sat down and were quiet . . . until I turned my back. In my peripheral vision, I saw an eraser fly across the room. The recipient of that eraser flipped over his desk, and the show-down was underway. The F words started flying. I froze in hyper-alert concentration; my test had begun. So much for my plan to overwhelm them with kindness. Taking a deep breath, I stalled for time to gather my thoughts. My conviction came back slowly and steadily. Stay centered; Model the behavior I want; Believe in them; Let there be natural consequences. I spoke with calm authority, nodding to the eraser victim, "Pick up your desk." Then, to the group, "Everyone look up here." It was the perfect segue to setting class expectations. It was not long before my students were getting noticed as models for appropriate school behavior.

Teaching was a high, and I was gaining experience at an accelerated rate. At that time, I also started socializing with other teachers who were similarly enthralled with their work. My new friendships were a huge part of my overall enjoyment of that period. I was experiencing an intoxicating combination of independence and stimulation. My world was opening up in wonderful and exciting ways, and I was reluctant to leave it even for a weekend. Blake represented a happy chapter from the past; I was starting to see myself as having moved on, and I wanted to keep moving.

I was pretty sure that I could accomplish two of the three objectives I had identified: I wanted to spend more time with my new friends, and I did not want to make that long commute often. My third objective, to come to some resolution in my relationship with Blake, might take some time. I was not at all sure what that would look like. I wanted a break, but not a break-up.

Early that fall, I made the bus trip out to visit him. Ordinarily, Blake would meet me at the bus terminal, but that time he asked me to take the train to Radnor. I remember schlepping through downtown Philadelphia at night with my suitcase, looking for the train station. I was lost. I tried to be cheerful, but I kept thinking I had only two days off, and there I was spending my precious time traveling. In those days the Greyhound trip took a full eight hours. Worse, two days later, I would have to do that same trip in reverse. It was in that dark time before cell phones, so I had to hunt for a pay phone. When I called Blake to say I was lost, he said, "Just ask someone; it's not that far." I was annoyed—and not just at Blake.

During the bus ride to Philadelphia, I had been reading Wayne Dyer's *Your Erroneous Zones*. I felt the book was addressing me—my conflict areas at any rate. I had scribbled all over the margins, noting ideas that had especially resonated with me. "Do I behave this way because I am seeking approval? How much of my behavior is determined purely by my own choices?" My current situation was a perfect example of what I had been reading. I was frustrated, and I kept asking myself, "What am I doing here?" I would much rather have been at home, socializing with my new friends. I recognized that my pattern was to seek approval. That bothered me. I knew I did not like my situation, but I couldn't see a way out of it—not a way that didn't involve hurting someone.

Larry couldn't restrain himself any longer. "You mean hurting someone *else*. You were certainly disregarding your own wants." Indeed.

Eventually I made it to Radnor, and Blake picked me up at the station. The next day we hung out with friends of his and did chores. I wanted to feel helpful and gracious; instead I felt tired and resentful as we weeded the pachysandra

27

around his parents' pool. I could see that I wasn't getting what I wanted. At the same time, I wasn't certain what it was that I did want. On the bus trip to Philadelphia, I had alternated between working on my separation pep talk and fantasizing about a different lifestyle. I was still trying to figure out the best way to suggest a break, waiting for the right timing.

I had expected that we would go out to dinner because Blake had told me ahead of time to bring something nice to wear. As I dressed for the evening, I was feeling on the verge of something exciting—my new independence—but I was still uneasy about how to cool things with Blake. We went to a charming restaurant on the Main Line with a romantic ambiance. It was nice to be alone with him, and I felt a connection between us. I remember looking at him and thinking what a pleasant person he was. At the same time, I wondered if, in some ways, I had outgrown him and was ready to move on. I was on a mission to design the new me.

A violin player came over and serenaded us. When Blake got down on his knees, I assumed he must have dropped something. When he asked, "Will you marry me?" I was too stunned to answer. Suddenly, there was a dazzling ring on my finger. At some point I managed to say, "Blake, I don't know if I'm ready for this." He countered with, "We don't have to rush into anything. Let's just enjoy the evening; we can work out the details later."

"How did you respond?"

I *said* nothing, but I was thinking "Holy shit!" On the one hand I was excited and flattered. On the other, I recognized that this was not my fantasy. Maybe in five years . . . I did not want to say, "No," and spoil the evening, but I was reluctant to say, "Yes." I was confused, and even had the thought, "Maybe this is what it's supposed to feel like." But then I reasoned that when something good happens, people are usually eager to share it. Therefore, something had to be wrong because I had no desire to tell anyone about this. I offered one more mild protestation, "Blake, I'm not sure . . ." He interrupted, using his pet name for me, "Lovie, let's just enjoy the evening." That got me off the hook for the moment. I needed to find a kind way to decline. The idea of saying, "No thank you," seemed so cold. In the end, I didn't say anything.

Blake seemed to take my silence for consent. He disregarded my hesitation and lack of enthusiasm. Apparently the idea of rejection never entered his mind. Or perhaps it did and he covered all contingencies so I would be swayed to accept his proposal. All evening long, I vacillated between feeling special and feeling numb. I kept thinking: Blake's a great guy; plenty of girls would consider him a super catch. Why wasn't I thrilled? Maybe uncertainty was a normal reaction.

After we left the restaurant, Blake suggested we stop by a friend's house to say "Hi." We had hardly finished exchanging greetings when Blake said, "We've got something to announce." I thought, "Whoa!" The problem was, I was only thinking it, not saying it. Once again, I was too stunned to speak up. I found myself swept up in their enthusiasm. When we got back to Blake's house, his parents were having a party, and suddenly we were the center of attention. Right away they asked if I'd told my parents. I said I'd do it later. The next thing I knew, Blake's mother had dialed their number and put the phone in my hand.

"It was a joint conspiracy!"

That was what it felt like, and it kept getting more complicated. Everybody was looking at me, expecting me to look like the happy bride-to-be. At one point I went off to the bathroom and stared at myself in the mirror. Big decisions were going down, and I wasn't even in on the plan.

The situation felt out of control. I remember thinking, "I'm just going to roll with it for now. Then I'll go home and I'll know what to do."

"What did you think was going to happen at home?"

I didn't have any idea. All I knew was that I was not getting anywhere trying to figure it out then and there. My hope was that I would be able to sort out my feelings once I was alone and had time to think things through. So I faked it. I put on a happy face and just played along with everyone else's enthusiasm.

"And you never said anything to stop it?"

At one point in the weekend, I did rally. I said, "Blake, we've got to figure this out." But that was the strongest resistance I managed to muster. I kept trying to form a decision by comparing mine to other relationships I knew well. My sister-in-law, Deb, did not waffle when my brother, Joe, proposed. I remembered back to the day Joe had motioned me over to where he was standing at the entrance to the gym. He was in the eighth grade. The majorette team was practicing at the far end by the stage. Joe pointed to a girl and said, "See her? Isn't she beautiful!" He and Deb started to go steady later that year. Joe said he never doubted that they were meant to be together; it was as if he recognized her as his destiny. Deb said that knowing her future with Joe was certain made it easy for her to get on with her studies and start her own business after they graduated. And they had seemed so happy planning their wedding.

It was like that for my mom and dad, too. Mom always said there had not been a doubt in her mind that Dad was the one. Dad had been so smitten with Mom when they first met, that he lost track of time. It would have been a trivial matter under normal circumstances, but they had met during wartime, and Dad missed the tender he was supposed to have shipped out on. He was considered AWOL, and was placed under house arrest while the Navy considered how to deal with the love-sick sailor. In the end, he was assigned to another ship and sent to Hawaii, in lieu of Japan. Mom was happy to wait for him, and wrote at least a letter a week to him while he was away. It was understood that they would marry as soon as his tour of duty had been served, and they did. I wanted to feel that kind of certainty, not the mixed emotion I was waffling in.

On the bus back to Pittsburgh, the woman next to me said, "Looks like you just got engaged." When I asked her how she knew, she pointed to my ring and said, "You keep looking at it then covering it up." I admitted to her, "Yeah, I'm confused. I'm not sure this is what I want." She advised me not to go through with it if I wasn't sure. Her advice made sense. The problem was, I really did not know what I wanted.

"What do you mean you didn't know? What happened to figuring out how to say, 'No.'"?

There was too strong a tide pulling me toward accepting. I had shifted from feeling negative to feeling ambivalent about it. Throughout the trip home, I continued to read sections of Dyer's book. It was all about breaking away from needing approval and following your true self. I liked the sound of that, but I was just too focused on pleasing others, even to the point of self-sacrifice.

When I got home I asked Dad how he had known that Mom was the one. He said, "You just know." He must have recognized my lack of enthusiasm because he added, "but sometimes you have to grow into it." Clearly, my relationship with Blake fell into that category; I would have to grow into it.

Over and over I reasoned, Blake was a good guy, never pretentious; I loved a lot about him. I admired his parents. They enjoyed a privileged life and generously included me in it. Blake was successful; other women would love the lifestyle that would come with marrying him. But I did not feel eager when I thought about getting married. I kept going back to thinking maybe this is the way you are supposed to feel when you get engaged. I was not systematically weighing the pros and cons of marrying Blake; it was a much more random process. After a lot of indecision limbo, the scale gradually tipped in the direction of marrying him. Before I knew it, it was a year later and there was a wedding planned.

"You speak of it in a passive voice. Weren't you in on the planning?"

Sure, but mostly as a spectator. Instead of overseeing the planning, I witnessed it. For one thing, I wanted to indulge Blake's family in an event they would consider suited to their social status, so I deferred to them on most of the details. And the big decisions were made on my behalf by my parents. In his enthusiasm, Dad invited over 300 of his closest family and friends. ("Exclusion" was not in my father's vocabulary.) In contrast, there may have been 30-some guests invited by Blake's parents.

So we were married, and it was a happy day for me. My father escorted me down the aisle of Holy Sepulcher, a beautiful old cathedral, for the special wedding mass.

"Blake was Catholic?"

No. That was another generous thing he did for me; he went through the appropriate training sessions with our priest in order to accommodate my father's wish.

After the ceremony Blake and I were giddy, and eager to dance. We giggled all the way to the reception. The band was great. I loved my dress. It was like something from a fairy tale, straight from *Modern Bride*. I wore a hat instead of a veil—I loved hats. I felt gorgeous, and everyone seemed to be having fun. And our honeymoon was a blast. We were off to a very good start.

⊰ **10** ⊱

Following My Passion

In his book, *Personal Power*, Tony Robbins described six distinct elements that operate for every individual: certainty/comfort, excitement/variety, significance, connection/love, growth, and contribution. The order in which people place these elements governs the way they make decisions and, essentially, the way they live their lives. The elements don't necessarily remain in a fixed order; they might get rearranged during different stages in a person's life.

The problem was, I had reasoned my way into my marriage with Blake; there had been no powerful common cause to bond us together. We were young; we got married. It hadn't been an inspired union. Blake was an easy-going guy, but comfort was not my most compelling operative. He was accommodating, too. For all I know, he might have moved his life around to embrace mine, but I did not ask him to. In the wake of comparison, after meeting Seth, I saw that Blake and I were on a direct path to certainty and predictability. Seth represented a radical shift towards excitement, connection, and contribution. That was the course I had stepped off of and longed to be back on. One way or another, I was going to change my course. That meant following my passion.

From the start, Seth and I had established a candid style of communicating with one another. He knew a lot about my relationship with Blake, and I knew a lot about his relationship with his girlfriend. We both often lamented that we could not have those introspective conversations with our partners. Seth became one of the elements I truly valued during that time. I enjoyed our interactions as colleagues for my three years at Highpoint, and I could have gone on with our meaningful, professional relationship indefinitely, but that wasn't an option; the school was being closed, and we all had to move on.

The thought of parting ways with Seth was almost unbearable. Intrigued as I was with him, it was way out of my comfort zone—and what I accepted as marital ethics— to actively pursue him. But Seth had begun to occupy my thoughts to such a degree that I began to feel disloyal to Blake. Often, when I was doing something or going somewhere with Blake, I caught myself imagining how much more stimulating it would be with Seth. I was concerned that I had cast him in the light of "forbidden fruit."

I knew from counseling that what we resist persists, and it had become obvious to me that I was resisting Seth. I decided that the only way I would get any peace was to confront him as a friend, confess my growing obsession, and thereby put it to rest. I reasoned that if we could meet and talk outside of our school setting, it would demystify Seth and allow me to get back on track with Blake.

Calculating? Naive? I couldn't say; I only knew that I had reached that tipping point where my discomfort had overwhelmed my complacency and awkwardness at being so . . . forward.

Anyway, we met for lunch, and we talked about everything: me, him, his plans, my plans. Our talk did not help me refocus on Blake, but it did help me come to a realization about myself: I wanted more from my relationship, and I was determined to go after it. I decided to tell Blake about my growing feelings for Seth. Blake's reaction to that information would either trigger an improvement in our relationship, or it would mark the first step on a different path for me. I was feeling emotionally alive again, and that was no small development. I went home to open up with Blake.

All along I had been withholding all my thoughts and feelings from Blake, so he had no idea that I felt something was missing in our relationship. When he told me to quit my job, that we didn't need for me to work, it was over. There was no way I was going to quit my job—my career was the one aspect of my life that I was certain was on the right track. That was the week I moved into Fort Apache.

⚜ 11 ⚜

Luck & Softball

My whole career seems to be charmed; things have always unfolded in perfect timing as if by magic or luck. I have come to expect success. After Highpoint School closed, I found the perfect teaching position at Oakdale High School. This one came with a different kind of challenge: one of the requirements for the position was that I coach the girls' softball team. What I knew about softball was far outweighed by what I did not know, but I had Seth's expertise to call on. I consulted him about setting the lineup, negotiating with the umpires, and running practices, and I used my personal experience to bolster my credibility as coach. No one suspected my less than stellar prowess as a player.

When I was a kid, I was by no means a serious softball player; nonetheless, I enjoyed the game and looked forward to playing on Thursday afternoons. My home town, Pleasant Hills, lived and breathed softball, and all the kids I knew played in one of the town's recreational leagues. I played through to the young end of the 14 - 17 league, which meant I was among more substantial young women— bigger, faster, scarier. In that small town environment, everyone knew everyone, and knew their averages from past seasons.

One Thursday we were playing the Steel Maidens, a team that had a formidable clean-up hitter. I couldn't tell you Kel's numbers, but most of her at-bats resulted in multiple bases. In those days there was a fourth outfielder, the rover, behind second and in front of the center. (They have since done away with the position—at least in Eastern 1 division intercollegiate play.) I don't remember Kel ever striking out, although every now and then she would hit a Texas-leaguer, and the rover would steal the show by swooping over and catching it on a hop in time to throw her out. Kel was easily 5'10" and massive. She didn't run very fast, but no catcher dared to block the plate when she came barreling down the line. Usually, though, she hit the ball clean over the outfield fence, or it bounced over for a ground-rule double. Kel must have played in the outfield—she had a heck of an arm—but I don't remember her defensive position.

When we were not at bat, my position was right field, not because I could throw (I couldn't), but because it was the least critical place in our configuration, and I liked that. I got to study the dandelions, read the advertisements posted on the five foot wooden fence, and smile at the people in the bleachers, free of the pressure of performing any obligatory fielding duties; I didn't have to run, catch, or throw; I could stand peacefully and enjoy the sunshine. Every now and then, I concentrated on the pitching and called out the count to the center fielder, just to give the impression that I was absorbed with the game.

There were signals I picked up on, and I knew to advance or move back depending on who was up, so I had backed up because Kel was at bat. I would have crouched, too, glove up and steadied by my right hand, to look more intent, except that I was paying attention to something on the other side of the fence that separated our field from the adjoining one. I noticed something like wild violets blooming along the base of the fence posts. Someone in the bleachers called out and I turned to see them, distracted from the situation at the plate, so I missed the "crack" of Kel's hit. I was turned facing the bleachers with the plate behind be, my open glove hanging at my side. I felt the thud on my hip as the crowd in the bleachers next to me exploded. By some miracle, I kept my glove closed as I brought it around to observe Kel's ball snug in it. Grinning, I held it up for the umpire to see, enjoying the amazement of my teammates. I'm lucky that way.

Of course that wasn't the story I led off with at my first practice as coach at Oakdale. I knew enough to pass for an experienced player. Besides, motivation was my natural strong suit. I loved the girls, they loved me, and our practices were such fun that varsity kids asked to play on our team. As proof of our chemistry, we went 13 and 1 for the season.

I have a thing for analogies, finding a way to connect any two subjects. Take softball and Seth, for instance. People always commented on how fascinating Seth was. They couldn't help being swept along in his banter. He made an unforgettable first impression. Weez referred to it as his "hit-and-run charming" mode. Seth had hit a home run with me. Then he just kept running.

That was easy.

⪪ 12 ⪫

Law of Attraction

Around the time Seth and I got married, I read Arnold Patent's *You Can Have it All*. The metaphysical message that I gleaned from it had a powerful effect on my thinking. Blending a scientific perspective with a spiritual perspective, I started considering all experience in terms of energy. I was excited by the statement "we create with our thoughts," and I was eager to apply it to create the life I desired. I felt perfectly in sync with Patent's message "First we must believe we have the power, and then use it in beneficial ways," because my objective was to operate from a state of unconditional love. I was likewise inspired by his statement "In order to master anything in the physical universe we must relinquish all attachment to it." I got that intellectually, but although I spoke the words with conviction, I was about as attached to specific outcomes as I could be.

Patent used the word "create." So did I, but often what I meant was "control." I was optimistically and enthusiastically intent on controlling my environment. I believed that through positive affirmations about what I wanted, I could create the ideal environment from which I could live my happy life. I remember reading about having more than 50,000 thoughts a day, but I failed to note that the vast majority of mine were centered around what was missing. I figured if I could master the creation piece, I would at last have the answer to my subconscious question, "How can I control my environment?" Over and over I rejected the answer that kept coming to me: "You can't."

There just had to be a way to bring all those moving parts into harmony. And when everything was lined up "just so," I was sure I would be perfectly content. Actually, I was pretty ingenious at maintaining my belief that I could pull it off. However, I was trying to fit round pegs into square holes, trying to squeeze everyone into the frame for snapshots of one big happy family. Compiling the album was always on my mind. It would serve as confirmation that all was well on the family front.

Besides being philosophically backwards, my efforts to orchestrate my circumstances to fit my mental pictures were doomed for practical reasons. Ree's husband, Gray, taught me a technique for analyzing feasibility. You can determine if a design is sound by carrying it to a ridiculous extreme. (If it works with one, will it work with a hundred?) When my circumstances seemed simple, controlling my environment seemed a viable plan; once things got really complicated though, I could not juggle enough to make things work.

When I first read *You Can Have it All*, and came across the term "Law of Attraction," it fell right into place as the label for a phenomenon I had experienced, but not processed. As a teenager, I was aware that somehow I influenced my reality, and I was content, then, to enjoy life as it came, without analyzing it. Years later, listening to and reading Esther Hicks and the teachings of Abraham about the Law of Attraction, I started to recognize the evidence of it in my experience.

According to Abraham, we attract what we focus on, not necessarily what we want. That pretty much summed up my situation when my relationship disintegrated—not what

I wanted. There was no denying that I spent a lot of time pondering my relationship with Seth. But really, I was trying to fix it, and even if that distinction had not been conscious, it meant that I considered our relationship to be broken. The final result was a striking demonstration of what I had attracted by focusing on what I did *not* want.

In the magical way that doors closing are followed by windows opening, I came to see that controlling my circumstances was not the way to lasting happiness anyway. The most liberating idea had replaced that objective: I could control how I *felt* about my experience.

The collective experience of my life led me to seek a reconnection with myself, so, in that sense, there was no succinct starting place to my re-alignment. However, one event did seem to be a natural beginning for compiling the story of my return to happiness. I came to think of it as my "first night". I pieced together my journal entries from that time.

⚜ 13 ⚜

First Night

If you slow something down enough, you can watch it without feeling any emotion at all. All you see is a stream of details, the little pieces that make up a moment. That is more or less what I noticed as I watched my husband of 25 years drive away. My heightened awareness fascinated me, and I wanted to hover in that untroubled state, indulging only my curiosity. I had the idea that if I could maintain that detachment, making choices would become effortless. But it was like trying to stay in a dream after you realized you were dreaming. Just the effort of thinking about it distorts it, and even as you try to reconstruct it, you feel it disintegrating.

The magical detachment was dissipating. I looked out the window waiting to see if some powerful sentiment would swoop in and fill the void. The seconds ticked on. Good so far. I loved the way thoughts seemed to drift into my awareness slowly and rhythmically. Emotions fanned out before me like a hand of cards. It dawned on me that, at that pace, I could make deliberate choices and influence my outcomes. Good.

A subtle hint of eagerness wafted into my awareness. Perhaps I had crossed that fine line between anxiety and excitement. On the one hand, I was relieved that my circumstance lacked the melodrama of a teenage break-up. On the other hand, there had been something exciting about having a girlfriend grab diet cokes and tissues, and rush to my side to comfort me as I cried over the yearbook. I knew Ree or Weez would drop whatever they were doing to be with me through this ordeal, but that option did not appeal. I was pleased to recognize both my reluctance and a kind of inclination. A compelling idea was brewing in my mind. Viktor Frankl said, "When we are no longer able to change a situation, we are challenged to change ourselves." If I could pull it off on my own, make it through that night without self pity, somehow some way, there would be a great payoff—and bragging rights to my success.

A shadow of doubt crossed my mind as I considered that my ambition might be just a spike of bravado; it might be followed by a desperate craving for sympathy later on. Not good. Over the course of my life there had been plenty of times when my positive attitude alone had altered outcomes. Okay, obviously my formula was not infallible. That situation warranted something more than a cheerful tone; it called for more substantive props. I needed a plan, and I wanted to communicate while I was in that open frame of mind. Given my circumstance, not feeling like a victim was a big deal, and I wanted to share my success with someone. From counseling I knew that by sharing my feelings I could re-experience them, and self-empowerment was a feeling I definitely wanted to prolong. I did not want my wave of optimism to collapse and slosh me up on the beach of self-pity. I had already put Ree on standby for the occasion, so I knew I could phone her on my slightest whim.

When I called, she answered on the first ring. I skipped the usual pleasantries, and dove straight in with my progress report. Ree set constraints on our conversation: no reviewing what led to the break-up ("If only . . ."), no jumping too far ahead ("Will I ever find true love?"), and no mentioning Seth. I agreed to her terms. Reviewing what had happened would probably have taken me down a path of negative emotions. That was a critical night for me; I needed to stay present. Eckhart Tolle said, "Your power is in the now." That would be my mantra. Analysis is not in the now, nor is speculation.

Ree and I brainstormed ways I could flood myself with pleasing sensations, distract myself, and keep my focus positive. I kept thinking of water analogies to describe my experience—beach, wave, storm. (I liked that tears were not part of it.) I thought of planning a "date" with myself for that night, considering what would comfort and distract me.

I made a list of "mindful indulgences":

- lavender-scented candle (the aromatherapy choice for calming)
- little desk fountain
- comfy nest on the couch with pillows and quilts
- silky pajamas and fuzzy slippers
- for dinner: salmon and spinach, for dessert: Lindt dark chocolate truffles
- island travel magazine
- comedy DVDs

Then I went out to shop for my treats. At the Redbox, I picked out *He's Just Not That Into You*, and *My Life in Ruins*, fully intending to find them funny.

Everything went well: the flickering light from the candle on the mantle, the soothing sound of trickling water from the fountain, the picture of an enticing tropical island on the coffee table in front of me. I curled my toes in the fuzz of my slippers and felt serene.

Once I caught myself reminiscing about a time a few months before when Seth and I were enjoying one another's company . . . the sound of laughter as we shared sushi on our patio in the sunset . . . the evening we walked into town to celebrate our 25th wedding anniversary . . . I pulled myself out of the tailspin. Then I called Ree to brag about my catch, and to find comfort in some normal chatter.

I loved the first movie and planned to fall asleep during the second one. Occasionally I dipped into self-pity, but each time I caught the slide and shifted my focus to something present. I concentrated on the pattern of my breathing, and petted Casper (he was curled up, purring on the couch beside me). Each time I recovered my equilibrium, I recognized an incremental improvement in my emotions, a personal victory. My overarching goal for that evening had been to keep myself in a positive space. I went to bed satisfied.

The following morning, brilliant sunlight streamed through the window, and I knew that I had accomplished something wonderful. That was just the beginning.

↤ **14** ↦

Choosing Happiness

One morning after that, I woke from a dream in which I was moving through a deep multi-layered picture frame from back to front. As I passed beyond each successive mat, my viewpoint expanded, but the glass was still apparent ahead. I rolled over and grabbed my journal, glad of the evidence that I had been seeking clarity even in my subconscious state. In my dream state, although I did not know how I would get through the glass, I was okay going along with the experience, somehow aware that I was seeing things from a broader perspective. In my awake state, I interpreted the glass as the barrier between me and happiness, and I was encouraged to see myself moving toward it with a degree of intention. Then it struck me as monumentally significant that I wanted to be happy.

Of course I got it that everyone wants to be happy. The thing was, I often had flashes of insight when counseling someone in distress. While they were *saying* that they wanted to get over something, I got that what they wanted even more was to demonstrate unmistakably that they had been wounded. The two were vastly distinct emotional starting places. I saw that the distinction came from a simple decision—not necessarily simple to execute, just simple as a concept. Lincoln must have come to that conclusion when he said, "Most people are about as happy as they make up their minds to be." My mind was made up. I was going for happiness. Admittedly, there were times it eluded me. I knew not to try to force it; it would come back in due course. I could distract myself and give the "Fairies of the Universe" time to regroup.

Detachment seems to be a way out of so much mental unease. I sometimes set it in motion by picturing my vantage point panning back in an aerial view. It starts with the room, then the house, town, state, coast, continent, earth, and finally I am looking at the scene from open space. From that distance, the details are obscured, and I feel unconstrained, fully cognizant and comfortable, yet with no awareness of my body. In that expansive state, I react to the ideas that arrive unemotionally, with varying degrees of interest. It is from that state that I do my most powerful creating. Much as I wanted to reside there, I knew from experience that I could not power my way in; I had to finesse my way in.

It was that way with clarity, too. When it came, and I was in an allowing, observing state, clarity seemed to spread out like concentric circles, expanding beyond my ability to process them. It dawned complete, and I experienced it as insight—until I tried to lock onto a specific piece. That little effort was enough to dispel it.

Every now and then I found myself in a dreamlike stream of reassuring thoughts. Gradually, as in a pleasant awakening, my awareness shifted to include my present surroundings, and an easy sense that everything was fine. I knew that it was all going to be okay, good somehow, that I was, at my essence, okay. That feeling so bolstered me that I was distracted, while it lasted, from the practiced logic of doubt, asking "How?" (How could this possibly work out!? This is monumentally bad.) Every thought in that direction, attracted a host of others, the "What about . . ." thoughts of loss.

No doubt my background in psychology played a helpful role in grappling with that downturn. I knew that others can hear your story with less attachment than you feel. It is easier for them to see alternatives, options, and different outcomes. In terms of balance, it helped me to try to view my story from another's perspective. When I pictured myself with choices, I inched along the teeter-totter of well-being toward the center, where I knew I was in striking distance of the delicate balance I was hoping for—the shift from feeling disempowered to feeling resourceful.

A Course in Miracles asserts that there are only two essential emotions, love or fear. I had a powerful conviction that if I could maintain my footing in love, I could override the negativity that often went hand in hand with separation. There was an evolution of clarity about what I wanted. Ultimately, everything culminated into one overarching desire. I was determined to be the source of my own happiness, and that first night alone had been testimony to my resolve.

⇥ **15** ⇤

Buried Wisdom

Somewhere down in my satchel full of advice was, "Don't dig up the past," so it surprised me to find how cathartic it was to write my story. Note to self: ease up on the advice. That said, I still felt a strong desire to share something from my own experience. I hoped it would be a contribution. I wanted to find an effective way to express it.

Larry's take shifted my perspective: "You need to set the stage for your analysis. What are you looking for, and, more important, why are you looking for it?" The *what* part was easy. I was looking for significant nuggets. Then the *why* came to me in a bundle of ideas that I tried to describe to him.

"I want to draw a map to happiness. I know that I have some buried wisdom, so I'm studying my life to find it."

Larry considered that a lot like trying to identify my "formula for success". He launched into an exercise he had done in a seminar: "We came back into the room after a break, and the chairs had all been set up in pairs facing one another. We were told to sit anywhere, but it had to be across from someone we had not sat next to before. Then we were instructed to tell our life story to our partner—in a couple of minutes. The leader called, "Stop," and we had to tell it again, but this time, we had to do it from someone else's perspective. The leader called "Stop" again. Then we had to tell it as if it were not true. We kept on having to tell it from some different angle. One version had to involve aliens. By the end of the exercise, the whole room was laughing, and nobody knew what their real story was."

My mind was still processing "formula for success". Formula, yes; success, not in the typical sense. More like formula for well-being. I felt a rush of excitement as I recognized a connection in the idea that came next. I had just spoken of buried wisdom when a related image popped into my mind. I saw myself on a treasure hunt, following the trail markers of my intuition. I didn't know where it would take me, but I was eager to follow.

⊰ **16** ⊱

Depression

Until my marriage to Seth started to come undone, my understanding of depression was not so much from personal experience as from observation. Back in college, there were always kids I knew who got depressed and stayed in it long enough to drop out. They got nothing to turn into something by default. And back before we had kids and husbands, Ree used to go through routine bouts of depression. In our frequent walks along the tow path, she shared a lot about that hopeless place. Fortunately, her depressions always seemed to pass quickly, but I was never quite sure how to accelerate their passage. Even then I was making notes for a philosophy which would clarify decades later: how to help people climb out of depression.

Now I can speak of depression firsthand. I know it tanks somewhere around hopelessness. Fear and despair and all their relatives live in the muck below. A key to getting out of depression is believing you have a choice.

In my work with depressed teenagers, I often ask, "Do you believe you can change your circumstances?" Larry counsels older people who have been entrenched in their perspectives—sometimes for lifetimes; consequently he has had to build up to that point by asking, "Do you believe that your circumstances can change?" Then he gives them time to factor in outside forces and warm to the idea of change. I usually have a more restrictive time frame to work in; I need to get them redirected and back to class before the bell rings.

I tell the kids I work with that depression is just an emotional emergency brake for when they start sliding down a slippery slope. They can view it as evidence of their fundamental will for self-preservation, that they are wired to seek emotional refuge. Even that little insight—that they produced a self-defense mechanism subconsciously—is enough of a step in the right direction to give them some emotional lift. I point out that by their willingness to listen to me, they are demonstrating a belief in possibility.

Distraction is sometimes the easiest way in. One time I was working with a young woman who felt completely shut down with depression, reluctant even to engage in conversation with me. Suddenly, a squirrel leaped up onto the ledge outside my office window. We both exclaimed our astonishment at the way he seemed to stand erect and stare directly at us for what seemed like minutes. After he had hopped off, I pointed out that during the interlude she had not been actively dealing with her emotional pain. Therefore, logically, she could rule out the permanence of her depression. After that, she opened up and the process was underway.

Often, kids feel defeated by the negative momentum of their circumstances and their lack of inspiration to combat them. Usually, though, they hear me when I tell them that we will start by slowing down the energy. I remind them that they effectively accomplished that in order to prevent themselves from sliding all the way to utter hopelessness. They sense the logic in that little dart of wisdom. So that we can transfer the responsibility for their success as efficiently as possible, I let them in on their progress at that point. They have already engaged willingness and reason. Next comes an exercise in deliberately shifting their energy.

I plant the thought seed that they can control how they feel, asking them for detailed descriptions. "What happens when . . . sunshine falls on your face?" . . . you pet a kitten? . . . you eat ice cream with hot fudge sauce? watch a funny movie with a friend?" I say, "You know yourself, and you have access to your formula for well-being. I will help you find useful tools; that's what we are going to work on together." Because I can read them and know some of their gifts, I share that clarity with them. "I see your (art, skill, intelligence). Right now you are stuck. Your self-judgment is skewed by your depression. Anchor your confidence to my vision, and it will transfer it to you in time." Then I help them rephrase their practiced negative statements into more positive, more powerful ones. The demonstrable success comes when they acknowledge their part in deliberately changing the direction of their prevailing attitude.

In the Fort Apache days, a friend who was involved with AA hung out with us and taught us some expressions that have come in handy from time to time since. For days when you're too overwhelmed to know where to start, "Make your bed, brush your teeth, go to a meeting." I re-worked it to, "Brush my teeth, walk the dog, go stand by the lake." And when my relationship with Seth was in the pits, I applied the mantra, "Don't think; don't drink; make meetings," as "Don't think about Seth; don't think about Seth; go stand by the lake." Water has always been powerful medicine for me.

⚜ 17 ⚜

Counseling a Friend

As it was coming together in my mind, I had the opportunity to express a lot of my emerging formula for happiness as I counseled a friend who was in the throes of a bitter divorce. As I spoke, I felt the conviction of my words so powerfully that I thought there was a real chance I might shift her bitterness, empower her to relinquish the role of victim. We were walking in the park behind the fitness center. The filtered light through the blue-gray clouds, the crisp air, saturated with moisture from the recent storm, all stoked my already high emotions to an exhilarating vibration. It was as if I had access to the universal flow chart of logic. If A, then . . . B. If C, then D. Whatever she threw into the conversation was irradiated to a higher energy in the beam of my clarity.

Over and over I heard her dip into the past and dredge up feelings of resentment. A quote from *A Course in Miracles* sprang into my mind: "The only purpose of time is to ease pain."

An obvious starting point from which to share my perspective with her congealed into the words I spoke. I saw it as a sort of "foundation question" for all quandaries: "Would you be willing to get to some place in the future where you do not feel upset about this?" I reworked it in order to give her a few moments to get her head around the idea. "If there were a way for you to get to some place in the future where you would forego the way you are holding this, would you want that?"

I saw her recoil from the idea of getting no retribution for her hurt. Essentially, she said, "I'll never forget." And when she said it, I knew that I had proposed too big a leap. I would have to lay a more gradual foundation. Although she and I had not spent a lot of time together, I knew she was bright and interested in spiritual growth. Our conversation that day would be influenced by her openness and my clarity. From my vantage point, I saw taking responsibility for my own happiness as a great opportunity, a shortcut to freedom and joy, but I had not gotten to that appreciation in one conversation. Our talk would likely be for her what all my early attempts to process those ideas had been for me, seeds. In her own time, and in a nurturing environment, her seeds would sprout and open to her unique light.

I asked if she were willing to examine her own timeline. Had she ever experienced emotional pain that she thought would not stop hurting, but in the end, had? She agreed, at least intellectually, and even voiced, "Time heals all wounds." But what about profound pain? Did that ever fully recede?

Just as I had had to decide in favor of happiness, I saw that, if she were to get herself happy again, she would have to make that decision, too. It was a lot to ask, but then, it was what she wanted. I saw that both happiness and hurt were decisions. If she insisted on focusing on her resentment, she would be making an unconscious decision to keep her pain alive. Even if she were to do nothing, to make no deliberate effort towards happiness, but simply cease stoking the embers of her pain, time would seep in and ease her experience.

Our conversation shifted to another fundamental belief. I asked if she ever got the sense that she was more than her body. My flow chart lit up "You Are Here." Yes or No. Either she experienced a broader self, an inner guidance, or not.

I asked, "Do you believe in the power of your mind?" Again, it was as if a light flashed at the decision point of that question. If "Yes, I believe the mind is powerful," an abundance of mental techniques would light up on the buffet of solutions. Visualization, meditation, distraction, recreation . . . If "No, I believe that things are as they are, that the mind is obligated to filter and interpret what comes to it," her satisfaction would depend on exacting a particular result, a penalty, a consequence. Retribution would be required.

I saw that the implications of her seeking retribution involved a lot of struggle. (Eliciting remorse from someone else was beyond the locus of her control.) By rationalizing her anger and mustering agreement, she would forfeit her ease. If she went that route, she would sacrifice her future to revisit her past.

I thought, but elected not to say, "Nothing you can do can alter the events that already took place. None of your future pain will do anything to alleviate your past pain. That's just bad math."

Until I heard the unhappy stuckness in my friend's story, I had not considered that the answer to the question "Do you believe you can change your experience?" might be, "No." In my work with kids I had heard only variations of "Yes, but I don't know how." It got me thinking about the importance of believing you can change your beliefs. Accepting that premise was one of the idea-gifts I received from Napoleon Hill. Abraham polished the idea with "A belief is a thought you keep thinking." I wished I had planted that seed-thought in my friend's mind. Just the willingness to accept—or at least to consider—that her beliefs could change, would be enough to start the process. After that she could nurture the idea to root among her beliefs.

As she voiced bitterness, my mind raced on to other outcomes. It was easy for me to get how she could apply those principles to transform her situation. I could picture whole arrays of possibilities that would please her if she would envision them. But she just wasn't ready to move on right then.

In what seemed like a download of clarity, the insight came to me that holding a future orientation was a powerful therapeutic tool. I felt fortunate to have it in my kit. Simultaneously, I got how I could have all the tools and all the skills, but not necessarily all the results I wanted. Bringing myself into consistent patterns of successful behavior was a process of unending refining. I understood that the real work lay in exercising a positive mindset.

The awareness had dawned in perfect ease. If anything, I felt relieved, even encouraged at the prospect of unending refining. Pieces of the grand scheme started clicking into place. It did not matter where I started. Happiness was not a destination. The real joy came from living in the moment. An unending stream of moments would steadily roll in like the surf. It was the natural order of life. I felt as if the pleasure I derived along the way was a matter of my determination. A key to happiness lay in my attitude. I believed that attitudes could be developed. I would nurture an attitude of positive expectation.

⊰ **18** ⊱

No Obstacles

That experience with my friend got me on a kind of roll. It made me eager to speed up my own progress, to get more dramatic results in my life, my body, mind, and spirit. My triad could use some balancing. Of the three, my spirit aspect seemed to be the most consistently tended. I had been deliberate in my habits there. In my frequent walks, I allowed the nature around me to bring my all senses to a state of heightened awareness. As often as I could, I drove to the shore and basked in the power and grandeur of the ocean, connecting to my most expansive self-awareness. Every morning I went through personal rituals that grounded me in well-being.

In the light of my new awareness, I saw that I had barely tapped the surface of my body aspect. I wanted to become more attuned with every aspect of my physicality. Off and on I had practiced mindful eating. There were foods that seemed to have an energizing effect on me, and those that I associated with inactivity. I could become more conscientious in my food choices. I had been strengthening and conditioning in exercise classes almost every day, and I was eager to develop a more robust physique. I could feel the harmonizing effect fitness had on my overall well-being.

It was time to take my mental vigilance up a notch. I was ready to uproot some flawed premises and bolster some fruitful beliefs. I wanted a clean disciplined mind, focused on my well-being. My determination to be happy hung like a figurative carrot at the forefront of my thoughts. The more aware I was of the goal, the more I was able to consider issues as obstacles. When my course was certain, worry, envy, and loneliness became mere detours.

At first, worry came in a torrent of fear-based questions. "Will I be able to keep the house? If not, where will I live? How will the kids take the news? Will I lose our couple friends? Will I be alone the rest of my life? Will I be the only one at the holiday party without a husband?" Once I had a bead on generating my own happiness, I had a different perspective on those issues. "It is a wide world; there are fabulous places I might prefer to live. I'm immune to judgment when I feel confident. I am entirely free to choose how I want to show up in my life."

Envy underwent a similar transformation. I started out with a desperate take. I could deal with not having Seth in my life, but the idea that he could become the enlightened partner I coveted on someone else's shift tortured me. I drove myself crazy envisioning him with another, living the lifestyle *I* was supposed to have had with him. Worse, I added self-recrimination for my blatantly unenlightened thinking. After I shifted my focus from external to internal, I became less troubled by resentment and more drawn to self-awareness. I started seeing things in terms of "How do I want to design *me*?" When I identified a trait or behavior that I considered desirable, I saw it as clarity about what I wanted to cultivate in myself. It became a little game: "Add that to my cart."

In the beginning, I felt un-connected in my empty house, un-related, un-defined. I had always thought of myself in terms of my relationship—at least in part. My expanded self-definition began to take shape as I established practices that contributed to my overall well-being: morning affirmations, yoga stretches, mindful eating, journaling, intense exercise with uplifting music. Gradually, I became re-connected and re-defined as I became more attuned to my relationship with myself.

⊰ **19** ⊱

Justification

Come to think of it, I had often felt lonely when Seth was in the house. Something was amiss in my logic. I had been hanging in there, believing I could transform our relationship, and I considered that confidence to be evidence of my optimism. But that got me wondering, what had been different before? If all along I had wanted things to work out, and all along I had believed that they would, what had gone wrong? Some big pieces must be missing. I was determined to reason it out. Was I or wasn't I an optimist? Absolutely, no question, I was. Had my optimism led to an outcome I wanted? Absolutely, no question, it had not. My core belief had been that optimism was inherently good, and would attract positive outcomes. There was a disconnect somewhere between that core belief and my experience. I needed to re-think that belief. Time for some more reflective writing.

Even though my closest friends and family questioned my willingness to put up with the blatant dysfunction of Seth's and my devolved relationship, I wouldn't yield. Larry periodically questioned my refusal to even entertain the notion of moving on. I was impervious to his logic. A pessimist would have called it obstinacy; I was an optimist, so I called it conviction. I was sure that I could bring the whole thing off somehow, I could right this course, get it going in the direction I wanted it to go. Another reason I gave for wanting to tough it out with Seth was that I had not been authentically expressing myself with him. I thought of Seth as a "final frontier"; if I could align there, I could be authentic anywhere. Larry pointed out the delusional thinking behind my objective, but I was not to be dissuaded. Seth and I were going to live happily ever after—*together*—if I had to cast a spell to make it happen.

It surprised me how easy it was to examine my story once I overcame neediness. I had gone through such long stretches of co-dependence with Seth that I was no longer even aware of my mis-alignment. The irony of my wanting to fix him was lost on me. Realizing how far I had strayed from my core principles did not incline me to self-recrimination; it provided comic relief.

I was pretty sure I was through with being co-dependent, but I suspected I still had a ways to go when it came to being . . . (I could not bring myself to say "manipulative") . . . directive. A lot of my efforts were what I considered to be benign, thoughtful even. Smoothing the bumps out of the ride for our kids, for example. Larry considered it all degrees of "creating in another's sandbox," trying to regulate their environment or experience on their behalf. I got his point. But when did being a protective parent taper to feeling confident that they would land—unassisted—on their feet? I felt the answer forming: when I started expecting that things would work out for them the same way I expected it for myself, when I relinquished the ownership of their outcomes to them.

I had been working so hard at being evolved, it was a relief to consider my story from an uncomplicated space. I saw myself in a continuum of evolution. I had always believed that I was a good person, and that life was supposed to be good. I saw myself as lovable, and universally loved. That pretty much summed it up: I liked myself, and I expected others to like me. Seth certainly had—in the beginning.

When Seth started to distance himself from me, I began a long and convoluted detour through insecurity. What if I was not as wonderful as I had thought. That premise launched a practice of doubt and comparison. Maybe other women were more . . . interesting? . . . captivating? . . . worldly? . . . accomplished? It did not take much time in that quagmire before I concluded that I must be somehow lacking. And because that premise was flawed, my subsequent reasoning was flawed. I set about trying to identify my deficiencies, determined to compensate for them.

As I reflected on what I had written, a Tony Robbins principle came to mind: "Don't ask your mind a question you don't want the answer to. It will scramble around and come up with something." I was setting myself up to confirm my feared inadequacy, and, according to Abraham, Law of Attraction would deliver precisely what I feared.

Before I started reading Esther & Jerry Hicks and the teachings of Abraham, I thought that what I attracted must come in one of two ways. I figured the majority of what showed up in my life was unplanned, the results summoned by my subconscious intentions or predetermined by all that I had lived. I believed I could *want* my way to specific desires through carefully designed lists and passionate statements. Obviously, I wasn't rigorous in my scientific methodology or I would have had to acknowledge that my results were neither consistent nor uniform. In some areas I felt utterly powerful and influential; in others, I kept re-writing my affirmations, and declaring them more succinctly, because I wasn't sure the powers that be got what I was asking for.

I came to accept that what comes to me matches me at the energy level, the vibrational level. Law of Attraction wasn't responding to my words, it was responding to my thoughts. The time I was spending in my deliberate positive intentions was a drop in the bucket of my ongoing subliminal thoughts of inadequacy and insufficiency. Law of Attraction responded to the dominant vibration I was emanating—insecurity.

However, at the time, I was proud of my attitude. I considered my sense of insufficiency to be a call for "self-improvement". Of course, the carrot kept moving out of reach. The more I tried to impress Seth, the less impressed he acted. And so it went.

There was one particular area in which I did feel especially confident back then; I considered myself farther advanced along the path of enlightenment than Seth was. Ree credited that to my "spiritual ego". It would be fair to say I was spiritually egotistical. I reasoned that if I could get Seth to see me as his teacher in enlightenment, it would restore the balance of our relationship (offset my deficiencies). At the time I considered my motives to be pure—generous even. I now see that, in my guru aspirations, I was subliminally discrediting my "aspirant" (Seth). Moreover, my desire to be seen as his teacher reflected the limiting belief that my self-worth was based in proving myself somehow.

One of the ways in which I felt more spiritually evolved than Seth, was in my general approach to situations. I believed: fix the attitude; then the experience will improve. Seth had a more pedestrian belief system: fix the circumstances; then you can feel good about them. I would point out that in that very moment, nothing was wrong, there was reason to be appreciative. He would counter that in that very moment, things sucked, there was reason to feel disturbed. I cheerfully pointed out what was working in our lives. Seth found my endless "glass half full" attitude maddening during tight financial times, in the face of his more objective "glass soon to be empty" awareness.

I cast us as Pollyanna and Godzilla. Pollyanna chirped about "fun family activities"; Godzilla muttered about "chores". I would have preferred that we work on tasks together; Seth insisted that we divide and conquer. On weekends, he dressed for battle, and set to tackling chores. It was Man vs. List, and every round was rung in with, "Next!" I tried to chose tasks in proximity to where he was working to maximize our togetherness. One time I was out in the yard at our house in Hopewell, raking autumn leaves, enjoying the crisp air. My reverie was interrupted by the blast of the leaf-blower being started up. It was apparent that I was standing, literally, in the way of progress. After we moved to Kingston, we replayed that scene in the springtime, when a carpet of pink petals covered our lawn. Seth put it perfectly, "You see cherry blossoms; I see work."

From my present perspective, I have a different take on that story. I pick up on the judgement I held. What I had written really translated to, "Lighten up." What I would now say is, "After I have my fill of blossoms, I'll help clean up."

Back then my feelings were wrapped up in co-dependence. I wanted Seth to appreciate me and to value my contribution, and I did not see that happening as long as I could not make him happy. My own happiness became contingent on his. I often urged, "Just be in your moment," to which Seth would respond, "I don't want to be in my moment; my moment sucks."

In *Men are from Mars, Women are from Venus*, John Gray wrote that men need to solve problems, whereas women need to receive appreciation and affection. I couldn't get over how precisely his ideas matched my experience.

Apparently, a lot of the magic of our relationship took place in my imagination. For one thing, as Abraham would say, I was making affirmations from a position of lack. They also said, "There is no point in speaking words you do not believe," but I had not yet gotten that distinction. My "affirmations" were actually a kind of supplication: "Please make this be right." There had been an unspoken second part to my "Please make this be right." Subconsciously, I was adding ". . . because it is not right." I was speaking things like "My life is a blessing," unaware that my focus was on the things that were missing in my marriage. I might have made progress if I had said, "I want to experience my life as a blessing." That affirmation would have set in motion the mindfulness of looking for what I did appreciate.

⊰ 20 ⊱

Re-Lifting my Mood

It seems to be true that we only accept what we are ready to accept. There had been one especially telling moment in which I was finally able to get Seth's refusal to see me as the intimate partner of his life journey. It had happened in the course of Couples Counseling, part of my no-stone-left-unturned initiative to salvage our marriage. The counselor had told us that it was crucial for the success of our endeavor that we committed to the project (succeeding as a couple). She had asked Seth to indicate his commitment. Instead, he said, "I don't know," whereupon she told us to contact her when we could both commit. We never did—either commit or contact her. When I heard his response to her request, I was surprised by my lack of emotion. I didn't really even react; I just studied the plaque on her office wall: "Above all else, guard your heart, for it is the wellspring of life. PROVERBS 4:23." Apparently I was ready to accept the end of an era.

Every little foray into negativity dragged my mood down a notch, and I wanted to get back into a better space. I would have to build up to a solid footing before I could begin sincerely appreciating my world. A good starting place was something safe and neutral, like "There is not a shred of doubt in my mind that I like feeling good more than I like feeling bad." From there I added other general statements until I felt the momentum pick up: "I like that when I feel good, what filters through to me seems better. Somehow I have temporarily muddied the water in my thinking, and if I just stay still, it will eventually clear. I take heart in the teachings that come across my path. I like turning my mood around. I'm getting good at this."

About there, I begin to feel aligned and positive. "I like the way I look at things when I'm in a good mood. Feeling good is my new baseline. My life is full of good feeling things. I am surrounded by love and beauty." And with that, I notice the sky, or smell something in bloom, or hear someone laughing, and I get back to feeling secure in my well-being.

Once I'm in that state of appreciative awareness, I want to take it a notch higher. My favorite technique for energy-shifting from Esther and Jerry Hicks' *Ask and It Is Given* is the Rampage of Appreciation. I run through all the things that are wonderful in my mind and heart in that moment. "I am so glad I have the tools to feel good. I love the way appreciation feels. I love my freedom. I love my work. I love living in a vibrant town. I feel so lucky to be the mom of Jesse and Jordan. I love having pets that remind me of joy in the moment. Im so lucky to have such good friends. I love feeling fit and alive. I love my life."

Ree had her own preferred technique from *Ask and It Is Given*. She liked to use Focus Wheels to re-tune her attitude regarding negative issues. She had filled notebooks with focus wheels, and I had heard her talk herself through them dozens of time before. It was tough to catch all the details because the process gained momentum as it unfolded. The end was sometimes a gush of positive affirmations. The start was identifying the troublesome idea itself—not the same as focusing negatively because of her absolute expectation of coming to peace with the issue. When Ree knew precisely what was at the root of her problem, she would begin re-orienting her thoughts around it.

One time Ree was describing something that had happened that bothered her, and she stopped mid-sentence, announcing that she was going to clean it up once and for all. I scribbled notes as fast as I could as she launched into a focus wheel:

> "I'm disappointed with myself about letting
>   things annoy me that I think ought to be
>   insignificant.
> I feel discouraged about getting so easily
>   derailed.
> I'm worried that I've lost my power."

She paused there so I knew she had identified the root of her issue. Then she set about changing her focus:

> "It's not hard for me to think of a time when I
>   felt powerful.
> It's not a stretch to imagine that I will
>   somehow recover my power.
> There have been times when my power
>   came back.
> Even if it doesn't come back right away, that
>   doesn't mean it's gone.

Sometimes, when I get past my worry, I get even more powerful."

With that last statement, I could she her shift visibly, and become more animated.

> "I like knowing I can get past a problem.
> Every time I do it, I feel more confident.

I believe that I can get my power back.

I expect it will come even sooner as a result of this work.

If this incident ends up making me feel more confident than before, then I'm glad it happened.

I can see that all my problems can be opportunities to re-align myself.

Being off my game is no big deal because I know how to get back on it."

And with that statement, Ree was clearly back on her game.

From the spiritual reading I had done, I knew it was all variations on a theme; it was immaterial which technique brought me back to the recognition of my fundamental well-being. Now that I had benefited from some successful practice, I accepted that if I felt off, my thinking must be off. But it was hard to identify exactly where my focus lay when my thoughts were scattered around a subject.

I often caught myself eavesdropping on my inner dialog. There were more—sometimes a lot more—than two in those conversations. Some of their voices seemed non-human. Thank God they spoke English. They could prattle on; I would ignore them. I started imagining my thoughts as an ever-flowing stream; I could reach for any one idea. I remembered hearing that we actually think about only one thing at a time. That made sense. Sometimes my thoughts seemed to come in an avalanche; nonetheless, they arrived one by one, just in rapid succession. I kept my mind on the idea I isolated for a little while, then selected another idea from the stream. Catch and release. That was the way I began to deliberately acquire the habit of mindful awareness.

If I caught a good-feeling thought, I played with it. Then I fished around for a related thought. Each additional good-feeling thought magnified my good-feeling reaction. When I snagged a yucky thought, I tossed it back and fished again. The appealing thoughts seemed to displace the unsettling thoughts, and any negativity that had my attention earlier would begin to dissipate.

⚜ 21 ⚜

Prismatic Light

Back when I was studying Cognitive Psychology, a classmate loaned me her copy of *Feeling Good* by David Burns. Even before reading it, I knew the theory that how we feel is rooted in how we think, and I was putting the concept into practice even before I had intellectualized it. Taking advantage of the fact that I could feel easy and invigorated even when I was only imagining something pleasant, I meditated often. In the process, I came to recognize those feelings as my natural state.

One morning I woke up "off" somehow. Slipping back under for another few moments of stillness with my eyes closed did not make it right, so I rose and sat in the sun and meditated. That worked. At some point I felt a frisson of some pleasant sensation, a tingling blend of excitement and ease. The closest image I could find was of flying in an airplane in brilliant sunlight, entering a cloud. I pictured sitting in a window seat, pressing my forehead against the cool glass to see as far out as I could, and then I was in it. There was a suggestion of moisture and coolness in the air. The cloud was composed of minuscule grayish-white translucent beads with opalescent surfaces. The beads swirled and moved slowly around me. My awareness shifted back and forth a few times from my chair to the cloud, each time accompanied by that pleasant feeling of some kind of energy.

When I opened my eyes, bands of sparkly light were evident all around the room in bright prismatic swatches cast by the sunlight through the crystal hung in the window. Tilting my head as birds do, I could get different colors to shine off facets of objects around me. The crystal vase was easy. In minute adjustments of my angle of perspective, I zeroed in to cycle through the red-orange-yellow-green-blue-indigo-violet array, sometimes skipping around in the order. I considered trying to be systematic about isolating each color, but gave over to the pleasure of the more random light show. Squinting my eyes a bit, I could get the light to play off the surface of my eyelashes, making rays from the mini stars extend out and retract. That experiment occupied me for a while. My face seemed like a solar dish, rotating in search of rays of light. Just by changing my lens aperture, I could detect different colored rays that had not been apparent before. Didn't that imply that they were there all along? I had the feeling that the implication was profound, but the analysis would have to wait; it was time to move on into my day.

⊰ **22** ⊱

Meditation

When Jesse and Jordan were little, in lieu of a bedtime story, I would sometimes give them a version of a guided meditation: "Imagine yourself in a garden, moving effortlessly in dappled sunlight under a canopy of tall trees. You walk along a path carpeted with lush moss and feel it spring back as you lift off each footstep. Tiny flowers line the path which winds toward a clearing. The subtle fragrance of orange blossoms wafts across on a delicate breeze. Spring peepers chorus rhythmically in the background, "crrk-crrk, crrk-crrk," and songbirds trill in the branches of the trees. The sound of flowing water crescendoes as the path opens into a glen. You come to a sparkling waterfall cascading into a clear pool. Smooth, sun-drenched rocks extend invitingly into the pool. You ease yourself onto a warm rock and dip your hand over the edge into the refreshing water. Rays of sunlight bounce off the colorful mosaic of pebbles at the bottom of the pool. Mist glistens on lacy ferns growing in the crevices of rocks beside the waterfall. A gray heron glides across the brilliant sky and you watch its slow, sinuous flight reflected in the surface of the water. The air feels fresh and you inhale deeply, letting your breath out in a sigh of contentment. All is well in your world."

Conjuring ideal scenes is one of the shortcuts I take to get myself in a good space. Often, I go to the beach—in my imagination. Stepping barefoot onto warm sand, hearing the rhythm of the surf, watching sand-pipers run in and out with the waves, all my senses are engaged. In this context I can truly appreciate contrast: I stretch out and bask in the sunshine until my shoulders feel hot. Then I dive into the surf and feel relieved by the bracing water. As I walk up the beach, the ocean breeze chills me. Then I wrap a towel around me and lie down on a warm blanket spread out over the hot sand. I visualize every cell in my body renewed while touched by the sunlight.

The imagery of the ocean uplifts me. As I watch seabirds flying across the water, I think about freedom. Even the gulls, wholly intent on finding food, appear to be swept up in moments of whimsical play. The rhythmic surf entrances me. Over and over, the waves rise up singly, swell, then break dramatically and merge back into the whole of the ocean. For all its distinction, the wave is never apart from the ocean; it is extended from the ocean for a moment, unique. Then it recombines inextricably with the ocean, to contribute some part to the subsequent generations of waves. The pattern repeats, although the substance is always changing.

Sometimes I visualize a tranquil beach scene; other times I imagine myself on a jetty that extends out into the ocean with waves swelling and crashing around me. Each scene has its mood. If I can not go to the beach in real time, I go there in my mind. It feels good either way. And when the good feelings wash over me, I try to milk them, to sustain them as long as I can.

On my list of places and things I associate with a state of well-being, flowing water is definitely at the top; around water I always feel renewed. Hiking in the mountains or through a forest—any nature setting gets me there. Likewise, laughter, intimacy, and stimulating conversation. I associate Vermont with all that I most love. Vacations there seemed idyllic.

✥ 23 ✥

Swimming in Vermont

Ree and Weez and I stayed close throughout marriages and kids. We hung out together a lot. Ree and Gray, Weez and Larry, and Seth and I vacationed together at least twice a year, and our kids shared in each other's rites of passage. When we vacationed together in Vermont, our families functioned as a collective; the kids considered the adults interchangeable parental units. One time Ree was out on a raft when her son, Daniel, got a boo-boo. When Weez and I came over to comfort him, he told us, "I want my *special* mommy." It was several years before Jesse realized that Uncle Gray and Uncle Larry weren't his real uncles.

In that environment of community and nature, it was easy for me to feel restored. At the lakefront, all I saw was water and mountains. With my children at play, my husband relaxed, and my obligations far away, I could give myself over to pure communion with the water. Swimming across the lake in Vermont became an annual event for Ree and me. It was a time when my body, mind, and spirit were all indulged.

Not all meditations involve stillness. We would walk slowly into the water, gradually slip down in, then begin gliding away from shore. By August the water got warm enough for me to immerse myself instantly; prior to that, it took time to acclimate. Of course, the kids observed no such limitations. They were already in, splashing around trying to avoid the "Lake Monster" (Gray) when we set off. They called to us to come in and join them. Ree learned to distrust their reports that it was "refreshing," and donned a shorty wet suit so she could swim without shivering. Each summer, the first time we got down to the lake, I marveled that just a few months before, there had been ice along the edges, and we had skied on the cross-country trails around it.

Soon it would be just me and the water; my parental responsibilities were suspended for those glorious hours. The husbands usually triangulated their posts to corral the kids. In a typical configuration, Gray would be in the lake chasing the kids under and around the dock that extended out just above the surface of the very shallow water, Seth would be in a rowboat fishing nearby, and Larry would be at the end of the dock, calling out sightings of the Lake Monster to the school of squealing fish-kids.

Once I submerged my body and started swimming away, there was no turning back. The view of Mount Carmel in the foreground acted like a majestic magnet, pulling me into the water. The children's laughter faded with each luxurious stroke, and was gradually replaced by the subtler sounds of lapping water and the rhythmic splashing from our strokes. Each time I got underway, I would think, "It doesn't get much better then this."

Using a Cayce analogy, God was the lake and I was a fish. I felt at one with the water. With the light and the mountains I was a small part of something enormous, connected to the earth and expanding into the universe. Words like infinity and un-ending abundance wafted through my mind, and I knew I was in the flow of love.

It was more than a mile out to the peninsula, and I only swam that far on summer vacations. Nonetheless, it seemed effortless, a prolonged moving meditation. Occasionally Ree and I chatted, but we usually reverted to the coveted rhythmic solitude after a few sentences. Ree liked to cycle through as many strokes as she could remember from Senior Lifesaving; I remained in breaststroke for the whole distance. That way I could keep my beloved floppy denim hat dry. It was the perfect gear in that it kept my hair out of my eyes, and allowed me to adjust the brim to regulate the sunlight that fell on my face. My choice of strokes also served to keep me (us) on course, which was a significant factor on windy days, when the currents could be quite powerful. Because Ree only faced our destination a small fraction of the time, she often zigged off course, and I hailed her when I thought she needed to make a correction. But, if she happened to be in the rapture of elementary backstroke (her favorite), her head tilted way back, and got swept by a divergent current, it might be a long time before she tuned back in and checked her course. I always felt a wave of fondness and amusement watching her stop and right herself, treading water and circling in obvious disorientation. Then she would spot me, and start a strong crawl to get back on course.

In one of my favorite memories, Ree and I were about three quarters of the way across when sounds of oars and laughter broke the aquatic trance. All the kids and Dads and Louise were rowing and kayaking across the lake, headed for "Jumping Rock," our announced destination. The joyful noisy naval invasion swept past us and we hurried in their wake to rendezvous with them on the peninsula. Having already scrambled up the flat face of the mega boulder they cheered us on from their high perch as we climbed out of the water. Ree and I sprawled out on the warm face of the sun-drenched rock to dry off. Then began the jumping competition. We had seen locals make bold dives way out from the edge, so we knew it could be done. Gray and Seth assessed the layout, and determined that the kids could do it safely, and Gray, being the largest of the lot, volunteered to risk life and limb to test his conviction. Like a trial penguin, he launched himself off and out and disappeared with a mighty splash. We could tell from his expression when he resurfaced that the game was on. One by one, each of the kids, and then Larry and Weez leapt out and performed some outrageous antic for the judges (Ree and me). I could not imagine how life could get any better than in that scene, on a lake with my closest friends and family, in my favorite place, surrounded by beauty and laughter.

Eventually the sun got low in the sky and the kids were ready for the next meal. Ree and I climbed down off the rock. The air was cooler then, so the water felt comparatively warmer as we slipped back into it. The rowboats and kayaks passed by us, headed for the beach. From the receding noise, we assumed everyone else had gone back, so it came as a surprise when Jordan quietly kayaked up alongside us. When we asked why he had not gone with the others, he informed us that he was keeping an eye on Susan. Susan!? Unbeknownst to either of us, she had followed us out and was paddling along (buoyed by her life jacket) like a retriever puppy, clearly proud and determined to swim the distance.

That was part of what I valued most about the whole Vermont atmosphere. Because we acted as a collective, the kids got to experience a kind of freedom that was not so easy to come by in a more tightly-supervised family unit. Every summer they got several weeks of the comparative autonomy that came with being supervised by loving adults other than their parents. We all valued that part.

⪥ 24 ⪤

Becoming Loving

You can pinpoint the grain of sand that an oyster makes into a pearl, but some personality characteristics don't seem to have a distinct beginning. Behaviors that get a favorable response tend to get repeated and rehearsed until voilà, you are pronounced thoughtful, or funny, or whatever, and you come to think of yourself that way. I can't remember a time when people didn't say I was loving. Nor can I remember a time when I did not consider my loving nature a precious gift. Love was the energy I wanted to take in and to radiate out. I envisioned it as a special kind of substance, and practiced exuding it at will.

When I was very young I imagined myself emitting a kind of light from my chest that permeated those I beamed it on. That imagery still works for me although I now identify the source as my heart chakra, and I call the emission "vibration". In the way thirsty plants perk up when given a drink of water, people seemed to perk up in my "beam". And, since my beam seemed inexhaustible, I decided to shine it on everyone I encountered.

Deliberately radiating love was my main way of communicating with my grandfather. He spoke only Italian, with a heavy Calabrese accent, and I couldn't understand him. I could sense his feelings though, and sent mine out to him. I did not need my father's translation that Papa had felt my love for him; I had seen his mood shift. I was happy seeing the change that came over people when I loved them. When I was a child, I thought of my intention as wanting to bestow my gift. Later on, I came across the perfect expression: I wanted to uplift people—all people, especially people who don't fit in somehow.

There are always some kids who stand apart in an elementary school yard. Claire was one of those. She was a loner; for companionship, she whispered to herself. She was younger than I was, but I felt drawn to her. I wanted to understand her world and to brighten it. One day I went over and sat next to her. We smiled at each other, and she spoke a bit to me. I felt love flow between us, and knew that she did too. Next thing I knew, someone else joined us. Claire was happy for the attention; I was pleased at being the instrument of her happiness.

⤙ **25** ⤚

Raindrops

When my brother, Joe, and I were growing up, riding in the back seat of our big old car on a rainy day, we would pass the time watching raindrop races. We used to bet on which raindrop would make it to the bottom of the window first. Joe was two years my senior, and very protective of me. Careful not to hurt my feelings by implying that my diminutive choice had poor odds, in kid physics terms he pointed out that the bigger the drop, the faster it runs. True enough, but speed wasn't my prime directive. For me, the game was all about inclusion.

Our excitement built as we watched each aquatic encounter burst into a new expanded entity. With rapt attention, we followed the subtle and abrupt alterations of route that ensued after each merger. There comes a point in the increasing volume of a drop when it sprints in a straight downward trajectory to the finish line. Sometimes that point came too soon for me; there was more I had hoped to accomplish before the race was over.

Joe had done two years' more raindrop-watching than I had, but I knew something I was pretty sure he did not know: I knew how to influence my drop. In the drizzle on the windshield track, there were tiny little drops. They were alone, without friends. I could hear Joe coaching his drop to ally with more voluminous neighboring ones. I whispered inaudibly to the shy little drops, "Hello there, would you like to come play with us?" coaxing them into our group. We zigged and zagged through the playground, assimilating the loners into our growing happy cluster. Joe often had to say, "No way!" as a sudden gust of wind drove his larger collective off the track, sparing mine, which then trickled across the flap at the bottom, and burst into the river along its edge.

When I was a child, I could get into that resourceful, magical space effortlessly; now I have to focus to get there. It was—and is—about being in alignment with love.

⊰ 26 ⊱

College Dream

When I did not actively pursue the theme of love, it pursued me. Off and on for many years, I had versions of a recurring dream, a nightmare really. It usually involves a couple of beings standing at the foot of my bed, solemnly letting me know there was something important that I had to do, or something crucial I had to remember. They did not say so, but I was convinced that I would die if the something did not happen. Worse, I couldn't remember what it was, and would call out to them as they began to dematerialize, "I can't remember . . . ," waking bolt upright, in my panic. I believe that the "something" represented me, my true self, the whole of my being which was starting to become veiled.

The dreams started after I received the "message" my sophomore year at college. I never found a satisfactory way to describe the experience. Sometimes I referred to it as a dream, but it was more like a visitation. Other people's descriptions of lucid visions, or waking dream states did not account for the nature of the interaction. Also, it was distinct from a dream in that I had not fallen asleep before it happened, nor did I wake up when it was over. Even though I knew that it had been a conscious experience, it was so far beyond my perception of reality (at the time) that I could not find adequate words to describe it.

It happened on a Friday night in the dorm. I had been upstairs partying with my friends, but I wasn't into it, so I headed downstairs to my room. Coincidentally—if there are such instances—that was the first time I met Blake. I did not so much meet him as run into him when we rounded a corner at the same time and came face to face. Later, he said that was the moment he fell in love with me. Because my encounter with him occurred on the same night as my pivotal experience, the two events are linked in my mind.

Around midnight, in the dim light of my room, still dressed for the party, I lay on the bed and closed my eyes, only to open them again a moment later when I felt a presence. I could make out the silhouette of a figure standing at the foot of my bed, but I felt no threat. Instead, I felt tremendous warmth, a sense of great comfort. I recognized that the figure was Jesus. When he spoke to me, I was flooded with a glorious feeling of well-being. His message was, "Everything in life is about love. The purpose of life is to learn to love." As I was basking in that marvelous feeling, a second figure appeared, taking the place of Jesus. This one was accompanied by a different, cooler feeling. I knew it was Freud. His words followed Jesus' words so precisely that they seemed to synchronize with and extend Jesus' message. Freud added, "Life is about solving sexual conflict. Conflict is not bad; it is a necessary part of growth. You will figure things out through sexual conflict until you come to a peaceful state of love." I felt as though I was receiving their message at several different levels simultaneously, that I was experiencing it in a way that was beyond mere understanding. Their message seemed to enter me vibrationally, and I experienced it as a visceral understanding, a knowing. Then a third figure appeared, and just as Freud had taken the place of Jesus, this new one replaced Freud. It was Darwin. He expounded on their message, "You will continue to grow and evolve through your sexual conflict until you experience love for yourself. This is your purpose—to learn to love, to evolve into perfect love."

As he spoke, I felt myself resonating in perfect harmony with the message. I listened in an state of complete clarity and ease. Then he spoke again. Gently, he said, "Now that you know this, it's time for you to remember; it is time for you to move on." For some reason, those last words sent me into an absolute panic. Primal fear shut down my ability to be present. I don't know what alarmed me; I heard only tenderness in his voice, and there had been nothing in the experience itself that made me feel fearful. Somehow I had interpreted that "to move on" meant to die, and I was convinced that I was about to be removed from this life into a different dimension. Desperate not to leave, I began to shout, "No! I don't want to remember! I don't want to remember!" I lay there tense with anxiety, gasping, "No!" until gradually it dawned on me, "Whoa, I'm still here; it's okay."

In spite of the abject fear of dying I suffered at the end of the experience, I felt a lingering amazement about the extraordinary way I had felt up until then. And whenever I contemplated their powerful message, I knew that it was now inextricably part of my being.

Years later, reading Dr. Brian Weiss' *Many Lives, Many Masters*, I came across an explanation that came the closest to describing what I had experienced. In the story, the therapist tries to get his patient to remember a past trauma in order to help her get over it. Part of the course of therapy involved hypnotizing the patient. In a hypnotic state, she described her past lives. With each transition to a different life, she experienced something akin to a flashback in which her whole life was reviewed as a lesson about love. That reminded me of the message I had received in my vision.

The problem was, the message had challenged my own definition of being loving. I had been told that conflict was a necessary part of growth, but I believed it was the result of being unloving and/or judgmental—the opposite of how I wanted to be. I rationalized, perhaps the beings in my vision had meant conflict was okay conceptually. Regardless, I was intent on avoiding it. The first message had been delivered as a loving reminder; subsequent dream messages felt more threatening: I dreamed that I had lost something or I was forgetting something vital. In my unwillingness to engage in conflict, I forfeited my full self-expression. What I was forgetting was authenticity.

My intuition was alerting me, "You are going to die . . ." The undelivered part of the message was ". . . if you do not express yourself." But I wasn't going to do that with Seth. I subconsciously knew that our relationship was not solid, and I feared that if I were to express myself fully, our marriage would dissolve. I chose illusion. And, for years, my intuition only voiced itself in my dreams. One in particular came to mind.

⤙ 27 ⤚

Sailing

Weez used to organize weekend sailing trips which we all looked forward to. We would drive down to Rock Hall, rent a boat, and sail off into the Chesapeake. Our usual boat slept eight, in various berths, some more comfortable than others. For instance, sleeping in the "V" berth often meant spending part of the night with your knees up, while your partner sprawled diagonally across the irregular space. Ah, but it also meant that you might get to watch the sun rise from your windows, depending on the orientation of your slip or mooring.

On one occasion the group consisted of Weez and Larry, Seth and me, and Warren, whom we knew from the New Hope Nordics cross country ski club, a brainchild of Weez's. Warren was one of those thoroughly inspiring people who lives life to the fullest. He claimed he started skiing at 70 because he was waiting until he could purchase lift tickets at the discounted senior rate. His kids bought him a piano for his 70th birthday. When I voiced surprise at not knowing he played, with an enigmatic smile, he responded, "I don't." Anyway, the five of us set out in the usual way. The theme song to Gilligan's Island suited that occasion. "Just sit right back and you'll hear a tale . . ." I wouldn't call it "fateful," but it certainly was a memorable trip.

The first night was uneventful. We ate what we had brought from home, and went to bed early. Instead of waking slowly with the sunrise, we were jolted out of our slumber in the semi-dark by a piercing shriek—mine. I had had another dream. That set the tone for the day.

It did not look particularly menacing as we headed out, but the weather got progressively worse. It was much too choppy to stay below, so we all hunkered down on the benches around the center deck. Seth was at the helm. Larry had his back to the hatch to best avoid the spray that occasionally came over the boat's sides. Observing that Warren was not wearing the foul weather gear he had brought along for just such an occasion, Larry asked if he might borrow it. Warren consented. When it did start to rain, Warren, the more experienced sailor, took over the helm. The waves got higher and started breaking over the deck. We were all tense. Acting as captain, Warren instructed us each to don a life preserver and fasten our safety tethers to the rail. Weez probably would have radioed the Coast Guard if she could have made it below, but the boat was pitching too wildly to do more than hang on to some fixed object.

There was no visibility, and we were unsure of our whereabouts. We had hastily dropped the sails a while back, so we were essentially adrift. Eventually the gale died down, and as soon as we were able to get our bearings, we motored to the nearest harbor. Cold, wet, and thoroughly shaken, we agreed to forego the plan to cook dinner on board, opting for the warm, dry, respite of the elegant marina restaurant instead. We changed clothes and debarked.

Once inside, we took comfort in steaming rich chowder and cool white wine. Waiting for our entrees, the conversation came around to my nightmare. Larry was adamant that

I should get therapy for what was obviously suppressed anger; that kind of potent emotion had to be expressed.

Warren argued that expressing anger was rude. He considered suppressing it to be the better part of valor. Larry insisted that suppression was detrimental to the bearer. Intellectually, I could agree with both positions. There was definitely something I was suppressing, and I would welcome professional help getting at the root of it, but I did not believe that the suppressed emotion disturbing me was anger. Even if it were, I did not think the solution was to express it; somehow I felt that would make it worse.

Larry was warming to his subject; he insisted that Warren was withholding anger at that moment. When Warren responded, "What if I am?" Larry urged him to express it right then and there. Trying to maintain civility, Warren said that if he were to express anger, it would be directed at Larry. Larry probed some more and got Warren to admit that he had felt angry at Larry for taking his foul weather gear, and leaving him to get drenched at the helm. Larry pointed out that Warren's problem was not being able to say, "No" or to ask for what he did want. Warren said it was difficult to say, "No." I had to side with Warren. Larry said that he asks for what he wants and he expects his friends to speak up, too.

Larry encouraged Warren to express his anger actively, and even offered him a model, "Fuck you, Larry, you selfish prick, blah blah blah." Warren said he wouldn't feel comfortable using that kind of language, especially to a friend. Larry countered that, especially to a friend, he *should* use that kind of language. He asked Warren if it bothered him when Weez said it to him, jokingly adding, ". . . because she says it to me at the least provocation." Warren considered that, but said he was not sure if Weez actually did use that expression. Weez set the record straight by turning to Larry and saying, "Fuck you for not giving him back his stuff when he needed it." That did it. Seth joined in the fun, "Fuck you, Lee, for waking us all this morning." Then it was my turn, "Fuck you, Seth, for taking up the whole bed." We were laughing and loudly firing verbal quips across the table over the general din of the restaurant. It reached a crescendo as Warren overcame his reluctance to utter the forbidden word. In some quirk of social timing, the restaurant fell silent just as Warren blurted out, "Fuck you, Larry, for taking my foul weather gear."

⤝ 28 ⤞

Pleasing Others

Warren and I were both what therapists call "Pleasers." We were accustomed to making sure that, first and foremost, we caused no offense. As did Warren, I believed that that was a positive attribute. It took the equivalent of an emotional earthquake to shake me into reconsidering my stance on pleasing others. Naturally, I wanted to be loved. I had wanted Seth to derive pleasure from pleasing me, which was not a problem in and of itself, but I had taken it a step farther. I had wanted each of us to put the other first. I knew that came under the category of mutual self-sacrifice, but it seemed like a reasonable formula for a loving relationship. Besides, I had seen it work. I had grown up in a family in which pleasing others, and having it reciprocated, was the unstated expectation. Since we all complied, it worked quite well, sort of. Admittedly, it involved a certain amount of guesswork and a high degree of flexibility.

We each tried to figure out what the others wanted, rarely focusing on what we wanted for ourselves. Deciding where to go for dinner, I might be in the mood for Chinese food, but I would suggest Italian, thinking that was what my brother wanted. Meanwhile, he would be speculating about what our mom might like. Sometimes none of us got what we wanted, but we were happy in the illusion that the others did.

Being focused on pleasing others was only part of what mattered to me. I thought back to my relationship with Blake. Certainly he had wanted to please me. But I knew I wanted something more, I just didn't know what it was until Seth came along. It turned out that the "more" was Seth himself. I wanted something beyond the easy-going kindness I got from Blake; I wanted more depth and stimulation. Weez had a joke about that theme:

> *Some women are walking around town, looking for mates. They come across a building with a sign posted on the door: "Inside you will come across a series of potential mates. These candidates will be presented to you one at a time. You may select any one from among them. Once you have made your selection, no further candidates will be available for your consideration. Proceed with caution up the stairs to meet the first candidate."*

> *Intrigued, the women decide to check it out. They enter and make their way to the first floor. There, they see an average-looking guy. No big deal. They read the sign at the entrance: "Candidate #1 – This man is willing to have a relationship. To view other candidates, continue up to the next floor." Unimpressed, they decide to move on. So up they go.*

> *They come to the second candidate. Again, nothing special. They read the sign: "Candidate #2 – This man is eager to have a relationship. He is gainfully employed. To view other candidates, continue up*

to the next floor." A modest improvement, nothing to get excited about. And up they go.

They come to the third candidate. Not bad. They read the sign: "Candidate #3 – This man has a good job. He is seeking a committed relationship. To view other candidates, continue up to the next floor." Interesting. They trot up to the next floor.

There they come to the fourth candidate. Wow. They read the sign: "Candidate #4 – This man is well-off. He is seeking a committed relationship. He is willing to have children. To view other candidates, continue up to the next floor." Very interesting. They hurry up to the next floor.

The candidate there is really good looking. The sign reads: "Candidate #5 – This man is wealthy. He loves children and wants a passionate relationship with one woman. To view other candidates, continue up to the next floor." Fabulous. They race up to the next floor.

The space is empty except for a sign that reads: "This exhibit is here for the purpose of demonstrating that women can never be satisfied!"

I could relate; I just did not know what I wanted. In some ways, my life with Blake had been picture perfect, but there was also evidence of our mismatch. For instance, for our first Christmas, Blake got me a foosball table and set it up in the kitchen. Although I probably responded graciously, the last thing I wanted to come home to on a Friday night was tribal beer-drinking and foosball. Nonetheless, I smiled and joined the game. But not for long, cheerfulness is not a substitute for happiness.

With Blake, I was aware that I was not growing spiritually. When Seth showed up in my life, I felt reawakened—kind of like Sleeping Beauty. I thought I had found a guy on the top floor.

⤙ **29** ⤚

Fairy Tales

Many chapters of my life with Seth had fairy tale overtones. The part where we met was like Snow White. Seth rode into my life like a gorgeous prince, with the thing that was most important to me—a passion for contribution—and he had everything else I wanted too. He was provocative emotionally, sexually, and intellectually. I was swept off my feet and out of my complacency. Of course there was the ongoing fantasy that we would live "happily ever after." I dreamed a lot, imagining that my hope constituted "planning for success."

Occasionally I thought of Seth as one of Peter Pan's "lost boys," and I fantasized about rescuing him. I believed that growing old together was a good thing, and I wanted us each to have carefree spirits through the process. I thought of fun as ageless. In my sophisticated analysis, I concluded that the problems in our relationship stemmed from Seth's perception that fun and playfulness could only look a certain way. I couldn't help feeling that he didn't see me as part of that general category of fun, and I fueled my insecurity by suspecting that he cast me as the mother figure, Wendy, in Peter Pan. I was desperate to combat that image, but I didn't know how to go about it. I resorted to my old standby, demonstrating love, but I was never certain exactly what Seth considered a representative gesture of love.

I poured through Dr. Gary Chapman's *Five Love Languages* intent on discovering which expressions counted the most for Seth, and to identify my own preferences.

> *Words of Affirmation* - Actions don't always speak louder than words. If this is your love language, unsolicited compliments mean the world to you. Hearing the words, "I love you," are important—hearing the reasons behind that love sends your spirits skyward. Insults can leave you shattered and are not easily forgotten.

> *Quality Time* - In the vernacular of Quality Time, nothing says, "I love you," like full, undivided attention. Being there for this type of person is critical, but really being there—with the TV off, fork and knife down, and all chores and tasks on standby—makes your significant other feel truly special and loved. Distractions, postponed dates, or the failure to listen can be especially hurtful.

> *Receiving Gifts* - Don't mistake this love language for materialism; the receiver of gifts thrives on the love, thoughtfulness, and effort behind the gift. If you speak this language, the perfect gift or gesture shows that you are known, you are cared for, and you are prized above whatever was sacrificed to bring the gift to you. A missed birthday, anniversary, or a hasty, thoughtless gift would be disastrous—so would the absence of everyday gestures.

Acts of Service - Can vacuuming the floors really be an expression of love? Absolutely! Anything you do to ease the burden of responsibilities weighing on an "Acts of Service" person will speak volumes. The words he or she most want to hear: "Let me do that for you." Laziness, broken commitments, and making more work for them tell speakers of this language their feelings don't matter.

Physical Touch - This language isn't all about the bedroom. A person whose primary language is Physical Touch is, not surprisingly, very touchy. Hugs, pats on the back, holding hands, and thoughtful touches on the arm, shoulder, or face—they can all be ways to show excitement, concern, care, and love. Physical presence and accessibility are crucial, while neglect or abuse can be unforgivable and destructive.

Fascinating reading, but it did not shed light on which love language Seth and I spoke as a couple. Other couples I knew fit the different categories more obviously. Weez and Larry often planned getaways to be alone together. They were good at Quality Time language. Deb and Joe were openly affectionate. For them, hugging was part of their daily routine; it could happen while one was preparing a salad for supper, or folding laundry in front of the TV. I wanted that on-going physical assurance. Maybe that was my true language of love; probably not, I was not exactly feeling fulfilled on the other fronts either.

It was not just the language of love that was elusive in my relationship with Seth, a whole realm of expression was missing. The caption "failure to communicate" applied to most of my marriage with him. I did a lot of subconscious rationalizing in our time together. When Seth was sick, I did not want to upset him. When he was having problems at work, I did not want to add to his burden with my issues. Ree used to say that I reminded her of Mr. Toad in *The Wind in the Willows*, "What are my needs compared with those of others?" I knew I came off as self-sacrificial on occasion— okay, often, but I felt things would go better if I weren't confrontational. On the other hand, my pile of undelivered communications was mounting; I had to lower it somehow.

⊰ 30 ⊱

Walking and Venting

Ever since Fort Apache, Ree and I have been getting together at least once a week, rain or shine, for a walk. Usually we walk along the tow path or the canal, but we occasionally opt for meadows, mountains, and even malls (in really inclement weather). In the interims between our walks, even though we often spoke on the phone, I used to save up my red-hot issues, knowing how much more fun it was to share them in motion than to speak them into a receiver. Within minutes of getting together, Ree and I would establish which one of us had the most pressing concern, and launch into discussing it with abandon. As soon as we arrived at some kind of resolution, understanding, or even just relief from the airing, we would move onto another topic. No subject was taboo. Way back, we had come to an agreement to leave each subject we talked about in an emotionally improved space.

Our walks were like free weekly therapy sessions. I looked forward to the exercise and the emotional lift I would get from regaling Ree with my stories, and when she reflected them back to me, I got to see them as entertainment. Ree would parody my role and exaggerate the dysfunction in colorful language, as I struggled to walk doubled over in laughter. I would spin a story of my disappointment that

Seth wasn't being an attentive partner, expecting sympathy. Instead, Ree would rail that I should speak up and stop being a capitulating wimp. The true problem was my lack of confidence confronting what I saw as a superior adversary. In the exercise and laughter I would envision myself effectively communicating my feelings to Seth. The thing was, whatever frustration or resentment I had felt at the onset of the walk had dissipated with the laughing and the venting. So, although I left each walk full of resolve to express myself, it was no longer fueled by resentment, and my habitual avoidance pattern invariably crept in to replace it by the time I got back home. My resolve rarely lasted long enough to end in actual communication with Seth. Fully expressing myself was something I planned to do when the time was right. The flaw in my approach was taking the moment for granted—all the moments, each one a window of opportunity.

In a dysfunctional way, avoidance was something Seth and I had in common. We even colluded on one of our avoidance tactics; we agreed we should not argue in front of the kids. That would have been well and good if we had believed that we *should* argue apart from the kids. Confrontations were never acceptable. Disagreements were to be avoided. As for rational arguments, we were waiting for the right moment. Obviously, we waited too long. In hindsight, my impassioned communications with Ree were dress rehearsals; I never made it to the real performance.

⊰ 31 ⊱

Anger and Judgment

Ironic that anger management was a significant component of my career, and I encouraged my own children to find healthy ways of expressing anger. My message was always, "Express anger responsibly; use appropriate filters." Yet when it came to my own expression, I applied so many filters that nothing remained to be communicated. I didn't want to blame or attack; I wanted to use "I" statements; I wanted to be an agent for change, to cause improvement; I didn't want my communication to cause hurt.

It is clear to me now that I was actively blocking opportunities for co-creation with my self-imposed restrictions. Although I was guarded against my own careless communication, I observed others' expressions of anger with voyeuristic fascination. Both Weez and Ree had a kind of self-assuredness that I admired. They could explode in anger—and often did—then move on to apparent closure in short order. I credited their success at wielding the lethal weapon with their frequent practice. Having had no prior experience expressing anger, I was reluctant to try it out on such an important subject (Seth).

Actually, I separated the subject into two distinct aspects: feeling anger and expressing anger. I viewed expressing anger as a variant of making someone else responsible for how I felt. I was adamant that blame was in the opposite direction of the path I wanted to follow. However, in my zeal to avoid being blameful, I banned any allowance of anger in general.

It was not that I did not have feelings akin to anger. I recognized my own resentment, annoyance, distaste, and other milder versions of the sentiment, but outright anger just seemed so . . . vicious. I made a distinction: it was not that I suppressed my feelings of anger; I prevented them from forming. I refused to explore anger because I feared that if I succumbed to it, my spiritual path would somehow be thwarted.

What I did not recognize about the nature of the expression of anger from Ree and Weez was that their outbursts were made from a solid intention to advance their relationships. They were expressing anger in a co-creative way. Their spouses understood that the bottom line was: "We will move forward through this."

One of the consequences I created by assuming that I could avoid feeling anger and simply intellectualize it was that I converted it to an equally pernicious feeling, resentment. Rejecting that as another character flaw, I covered my resentment with denial. So I had a lot of untangling to do to get myself to authentic communication.

One of my favorite theories from my counseling training was Albert Ellis's Rational Emotive Theory. I utilized it liberally to help clients process their emotions. One of Ellis's premises is that we should not judge any emotion as good or bad; it is the thoughts and stories we attach to our emotions that distort them. (Curiously, I was obliged to modify that premise in order to justify my own judgement about anger.)

From *A Course in Miracles*, I resonated with the message that anger is an illusion, based in a false belief that you have been wronged, and that you are in no way responsible for it. Taking responsibility for my circumstances was surely the high road to enlightenment, at least Deepak Chopra thought so, "I will take responsibility for my situation and for all those events I see as problems. I know that taking responsibility means not blaming anyone or anything for my situation." Also, anger seemed to be a form of judgment, and I was certain that my path was not to judge things as right or wrong, but to look at them as catalysts for growth.

Being loving and non-judgmental were the keys to my spirituality. Of that I was certain. Part of what I liked so much about my profession was getting to put my spirituality into practice daily. As a counselor, I was trained to seek "unconditional positive regard," and not to be judgmental. When I got stuck and felt myself beginning to judge, I recalled a story from a CD I used to listen to on my drive in to work: *The Farmer's Son.*

> *Once there was a farmer who had a son and a horse. One day his horse ran away. His neighbors came to console him, "It's such bad luck that your horse ran away." But the farmer just smiled and said, "Who can say if it's good luck or bad luck." The neighbors thought that was silly, "Of course it's bad luck!" Within a week the horse returned and with him were 20 horses. The neighbors were impressed, "It's such good luck that your horse brought you 20 more horses!" But the farmer just smiled and said, "Who can say if it's good luck or bad luck." The neighbors thought he was foolish, "Of course it's good luck!" Within a week the farmer's son went out to tend the new horses and broke his leg. The neighbors felt sorry for him, "It's such bad luck that your son*

broke his leg." But the farmer just smiled and said, "Who can say if it's good luck or bad luck." The neighbors shook their heads, "Of course it's bad luck!" Within a week an army came through the village where the farmer lived. They took with them all the able-bodied young men, but they left the farmer's son behind because his leg was broken.

Of course I don't typically say it out loud, but often, in my daily practice, I think "Who can say . . . ?" when kids present their situations from a certain perspective. I *do* say, "Sometimes there is a hidden opportunity in a situation," and that is often enough to shift the conversation toward possibility. People are more resourceful when they focus on what is possible. From my vantage point, I see them as capable of effecting a positive outcome. My work is to fan the embers of that expectation in them as well.

⇥ 32 ⇤

Beyond Fear of Negativity

I made a game of finding the positive aspects of people or situations. It was a self-rewarding challenge. When I was younger, my self-assigned purpose had been to make people happy; later, I clarified my desire: I wanted to be an uplifter of people.

Somewhere along the way in my relationship with Seth, my pure positive intention had become laced with agenda. I had wanted more than his happiness; I had wanted him to credit me with his happiness. Big difference. Despite the terms I was using, what I really had in mind was a desire to rescue him. Instead of wanting to receive the fairy tale kiss from the prince, I wanted to transmit the kiss that reawakened him, that returned him to the state in which he appreciated my essence.

In effect, my attitude was disempowering. Even the word makes me shudder. Not at all what I wanted. I would have to strip the heroine element out of my aspirations and interact with others on an equal footing. When I shed my guru persona, I would see us as similarly empowered. I wanted to hold others as equally capable of connecting with Infinite Intelligence and equally capable of tapping into the joy of well-being. The inspiration made me think of my grade school

American history class. I wanted to "assume among the powers of the earth, the separate and equal station to which the Laws of Nature and of Nature's God entitle . . ." each of us. Funny that the source of my insight should be a document about separation. Being non-judgmental was a cornerstone in my foundation; no wonder our house had toppled.

I recognized a step in logic along the path to realigning on that. I had to get past my own fear of negativity—and not just where Seth was concerned. I had to go from hoping this was a universe of well-being to knowing it was, and not just my well-being, everyone's well-being. From there I could see the logic of how things I had perceived as negative had helped me clarify my desire and had made me want to seek alignment all the more. It had to be that way for us all. I had to stop protecting others from their own negative experiences and grant them the sovereignty of their own decisions.

I started to operate from that insight with the kids (and their parents) who came to me in a panic around college decision time when they got denied by their top choice schools. I could communicate powerfully because my message was backed by strong conviction. "Find a way to make yourself okay with the next school on your list. Ultimately, your well-being does not come from any external factors. Find a way to create what you are inspired to create. The name of your school cannot give you the worthiness you seek; that has to come from within, and no perceived obstacle can block your path if you are determined to be successful." I told them not to sweat the process, just to follow their instincts and make adjustments as things unfolded along the way. My walls became plastered with Thank You notes, and I had celebrated countless times with kids who came back for a visit after a year at their "not chosen" school, delighted that things had *not* gone according to their original plans.

⚔ 33 ⚔

Marriage, Worthiness, and Loving

Since I believed in eternal expansion, and evolution, did it even make sense to try to coordinate all of that flux with one individual? Was the whole institution of marriage just a practical attempt at stabilizing something naturally precarious? But the viability of marriage was not really the crux of the issue I was grappling with. Besides, I certainly valued familiarity and intimacy, shared responsibility, consistency and compatibility, so marriage definitely appealed to me as a worthy pursuit. The problem was that I had lumped something pernicious into the mix of my matrimonial expectations—something that was completely out of alignment with my core principles. I had been trying to get something from my spouse that I was supposed to have given myself—worthiness. Before I could be in sync with love in all aspects of my life, I would have to align with the inherent worthiness of my being.

I love it when an answer pops into my mind long after I have taken my mind off the question. Part of the fun of following my thoughts is correlating the snapshots that make it into my awareness with the original line of thinking that attracted them. A while back I had asked the question, "What is the actual anatomy of loving?" Images from fond memories flooded into my mind. Dad gazing at Mom on their anniversary, his look of profound admiration. Mom watching Jesse and Jordan at our family picnic, a mixture of pride and delight in her eyes. In my mental archives, I had filed those images in a vast folder marked "love." I felt my energy shift into resonance with the distinct vibration of a particular recollection of love. The scene was from Ree's and Gray's wedding.

Sunlight was coming through the mist over the pond where the wedding guests were seated at Weez's and Larry's place in New Hope. As host, Larry was in the first row. For the close of the ceremony, Ree's sister, Lisa, had recited something based closely on *A Midsummer Night's Dream*. She came to the line about blessing the host, and as she spoke the words, she showered Larry with flower petals. He tipped back his head to let the petals fall on his face, glowing with obvious pleasure at Lisa's gesture. Ree and Gray looked positively radiant, standing on the tiny dock Weez and Larry had built for the occasion. The beauty of the scene washed over me. I thought over what I had read earlier in the ceremony, "Love is not love which alters when it alteration finds." Even as I was speaking the words, I knew that I wanted to revisit the idea at leisure, to see if it was simply lovely poetry, or if it was what I believed about love.

For starters, what about the distinction of being *in* love versus loving? I came up with two parameters. The first was that in love was an arbitrary point on each individual's scale. You were in it when you reached a critical amount of positive attention for another. The second was based on intensity, not quantity. You were in it when you felt a surge of affection or energy when the other sporadically came into your thoughts. Rendezvous in that zone were forms of passion, filled with childlike, generous energy. But sometimes I thought love had a lot more to do with behavior than with emotion.

It occurred to me that I could be more purposeful in procuring information, so I found a copy of *Gray's Anatomy* and looked up "Heart". The index directed me to page 640. The heading read, "The Nervous System." That was odd. Maybe all along I had mis-categorized "cardio-" things, but I soon concluded that it must have been a typo. I had assumed there would not be mistakes in such a widely sanctioned tome. Interesting . . . but off topic. What I sought was actually on page 460. I had expected the pictures would set off some kind of sympathetic vibration, and I would describe the sensations, as if I were a mad scientist in an old movie, transcribing my observations for posterity. The *Twilight Zone* theme was going off in my mind. Already this process was saturated with aberrant thinking: self-doubt, false credit, unfulfilled expectation. There was something I wanted, but I wasn't going to find it at this time, on this path, in this way. I would have to check a more reliable source, my intuition.

Closing my eyes, I tuned to my breathing, and eased my thoughts over to a recollection of loving. I chose one of my easiest subjects, loving my cat. The warmth started to circulate. Data entry # 1: "Sensation of temperature change . . . increase. Comfort—not exactly . . . more like ease. Shift in awareness—more general . . . release of distractions, cessation of stress." I would not make any more effort to document it; I would just bask there for a while.

⪥ **34** ⪤

Sea Chanties

It was late in the day when I recognized what I had been humming off and on throughout the morning. It was one of the sea chanties Warren and Ree would sing to us as we sailed around the Chesapeake Bay. Warren was the captain, not just because the ship was signed out in his name, but because he loved being involved with every aspect of sailing. Ree, on the other hand, gladly took the title "coffee mate" since food preparation was her preferred maritime duty. When we were way out in the bay, Warren at the helm, and Ree up from the galley, the two of them would commence to sing for what seemed like an hour straight without repeating a song. The rest of us would join in on the choruses we picked up as they sang. Some of the lyrics never failed to make me smile.

A capital ship for an ocean trip was the Walloping Window Blind.
No gale that blew dismayed her crew or troubled the captain's mind.
The man at the wheel was made to feel contempt for the wildest blow,
And it often appeared when the weather had cleared that he'd been in his bunk below.

Being out on the water with the the sun on my face and the wind blowing back my hair, enjoying my friends' repertoire of a cappella tunes, was pure pleasure. When we went out for three day weekends, on one of the nights we sailed into some harbor, rented a mooring, and caught a shuttle boat to shore for a meal of steamed crabs and corn on the cob. After a day in the elements, we all turned in relatively early. Some of us took sleeping bags up to the bow to fall asleep under the stars. It was magically quiet; the only sounds came from the tinkling of the laniards of the furled sails against the mast. We would wake in the cool morning air and watch the sun rise while still in the warmth of our sleeping bags.

✦ 35 ✦

Weez

Sailing was just one of many activities Weez brought into our lives. She is an accomplisher, a creator. Having Weez in my life was like having my own personal events coordinator, bringing me a stream of activities involving elements I loved: nature, camaraderie, robust activity. Weez was eager to sample all kinds of experiences. One day I came home to find her lying on the living room floor, arms spread wide out, with an ecstatic expression on her face. She signaled me to wait, then gradually eased back into a sitting position, and let out a long breath. She had been getting herself mentally prepared for her first skydiving adventure, that she had scheduled for the coming weekend.

When I try to describe Weez, it ends up as a gush of admirable qualities. I wish I could write in 3D; I would compose a beautiful sphere of acknowledgment. Since I must choose, spontaneity wins the toss. That works; it is a label that would delight Weez—she is easily delighted. Energy. Ease. Images pop up of Weez in flannel, with mussed hair, cupping a mug of steaming coffee, breathing in the fresh mountain air at a venue she procured to share with friends and family. Generous, too. When Weez discovers something wonderful or fun, she automatically begins strategizing ways to make it available to her huge circle of friends and loved ones. That means she is constantly plotting some gesture of sharing, because she is constantly finding joy in her world.

Weez is a connector. She makes things happen, and brings people together to make even bigger things happen. Her organizational debut was founding a cross-country ski club. There were maybe five charter members, including Ree and Warren, at the first meeting of the New Hope Nordics. It was up to thirty when I joined the following year. (It is still going strong twenty-some years later.) Best of all, Weez organized ski trips, each one more fun than the previous one. However, one particular trip to Mount Snow, in WhiteHall, took the prize for "Most Exciting".

Lisa, and I had skied up to a chalet and were sitting outside on benches in the sun, trail maps spread out, planning our route for the afternoon. The tantalizing smell wafting from the kitchen induced us to forego the trail mix we had packed for lunch in favor of a memorable lentil stew in a "bowl" carved out of Vermont sourdough. Lisa and I speak of it to this day. We had a few hours before our scheduled departure, so we planned to take a long winding trail described as "moderately challenging, with rolling hills" that led back to the lodge where the bus was to meet us. Weez and Ree grabbed a quick bite for sustenance, then took off, headed for some quadruple diamond kryptonite level trail. They are both athletically inclined; Weez was a cross-country ski instructor at a bunch of places; Ree was a riding instructor at Centenary College. Although I was always the first one on the slopes, and the last one off, they could cover the same distance in half the time.

It was a glorious day: brilliant sunshine, new snow, perfect temperature. About two hours later, Lisa and I concluded that we were . . . (I was reluctant to say lost) . . . unsure of our bearings. As we stood at the juncture of two trails, studying our trail maps, Weez and Ree came barreling into the intersection. Mutual surprise and delight was followed by confusion. "What are you doing here!? What are you doing here!?". None of us knew where we were on the map, and we agreed that we might be cutting it too close if we retraced either of our routes. We chose a new course that we hoped was the most direct route back to the bus, and all took off together at a brisk pace. The trail got more steep and winding. The trees became more dense. After a while it was obvious that we were not on a trail; we were skiing through a forest. It was impossible to follow the person in front of you because we were all too focused on trying to keep both skis on the same side of the trees we were flying past. Whoops and shrieks and laughter came pouring down the slope as the four of us zigged and speared our way around the arboreal obstacle course.

When we burst out of the trees onto an open field, the lodge was nowhere to be seen. Clearly, we were no longer even on the touring center grounds. Worse, we were running out of time and anxious about getting left behind by the bus—especially awkward as Weez had chartered it. Then Weez spotted something. Beyond the field lay a road and a small building with a police car parked next to it. "Head for the road!" Adrenaline pumping, we all began to bound, herringbone, and galumph across the field toward the road in a Nordic reenactment of Picket's Charge. Weez and Ree arrived first, jumped out of their skis, and ran up to the police car.

The young officer, who had been enjoying a quiet moment alone in the sun, was powerless to resist the two breathless beauties who stormed him. But how could he help, having no ski rack? Ree sprang into Field Marshal mode, directing Lisa and me to place our skis in a pile in line with the side of the car, get in the back seat of the vehicle, roll down the window on the passenger side, and hold our arms straight out through it. She told Weez to ride shotgun and do likewise. The officer was instructed to remain in the driver's seat and await her signal; he complied, still baffled at how we had gotten so far from the ski center. Ree lifted the back end of the stack of skis and poles, and set it across our outstretched arms, then she set the front end of the stack across Weez's arms, and ran around to sit in the seat behind the driver. It was like a rodeo stunt. She called, "Ready!" and away we went, cold air blasting from the open windows on the passenger side of the police car. As we approached the lot where the bus was loading, Weez asked the officer if he would be kind enough to drop us off a block away, so that we could make an inconspicuous arrival, thus preserving our dignity and maintaining the confidence of the other participants on Weez's trip. And we almost pulled it off. However, as the bus pulled out of the lot, one of the aforementioned participants asked, "Did I see you guys get out of a police car back there?" Thus we were obliged to disclose our saga to the rapt audience. What Weez forfeited in the confidence of her participants, she more than recouped in their admiration for her sense of adventure.

Another of Weez's organizational coups was founding the Swan Creek Rowing Club. Larry did crew in college, and stayed tight with his crew buddies throughout the years. It was something he had loved and wanted to share with her. Weez tried it and loved it, so she came up with a way to make sculling more accessible. I had only to hear her describe the sport to know it was for me. First of all, it involves being on water. But better than in a kayak or canoe, it felt closer to the water, more sensual. I liked all the aspects of it. Controlling the stillness, the sound of the strokes, focusing on balance, gliding . . . Not long ago, I was talking with a woman and discovered that she was a member of that club, too. When I told her Weez was a close friend, she asked, "Did you know there was a boat named a boat after her?" I did know; I have been out in that boat at twilight, with a full moon rising.

⊰ 36 ⊱

Decisiveness

Full moons, crescent moons, all phases of the moon delight me. Friends know to text me at any hour when they see an interesting moonscape. When I am out walking Buddy at night, we often hop in the car and drive down to the lake to get an unimpeded view of my beloved luminary. Buddy is happy to extend his nightly excursion for any reason. Although he has never howled at the moon, I'm convinced he enjoys it. Probably he picks up on my raised energy on moonlit nights. One time Jesse asked Lisa's husband, Pat (a biologist) why coyotes howl at the moon. Pat replied, "They don't howl at the moon; they howl. Artists create the silhouette images that make the two subjects appear linked." Jesse loved it; I preferred to think of coyotes as fellow moon-worshipers.

Given my preoccupation with all things lunar, it is natural that I assign some special power to the lunar cycle. I think of it as the perfect time frame for a new philosophical insight. With each cycle comes a theme. As it emerges distinct from the soup of my general intentions, finding a label for it becomes a significant part of the game. Then I get to watch for it to show up in my experience. One month's theme was decisiveness. Even the word excited me; I could hardly wait for the full moon that marks the culmination of the cycle. Evidence of decisiveness—and its absence—was all around me, in my own behavior and in the conversations and stories that came my way.

Just a thought: did I decide to be indecisive? Larry said I was indecisive because I could not bear the idea of missing out on something good. That idea fit in with an emotionally resounding click, and it explained so much. First of all, it meant that I was not making choices freely, I was choosing from limitation. Once again I set to re-thinking the whole thing.

One day back at Fort Apache, Weez had just finished a seminar, and was eager to share her insight with me. She held out her two hands, as if holding imaginary ice cream cones, and asked me, "Chocolate or vanilla?" I chose chocolate. Weez asked me why, and I responded that I preferred chocolate. Then it got weird. Weez said, "No, *choose*," and started over, "Chocolate or vanilla?" I chose vanilla. Weez asked why. "Because last time I chose chocolate, and that wasn't it." Again she offered the ice cream, and again I gave my reason. Weez's eagerness for my breakthrough had a direct correlation to my frustration at not getting it. Finally the moment came (having abandoned hope of reasoning the thing out), when I chose a flavor, then answered the question "Why?" with, "Just because." Weez's whoop heralded my successful arrival at the point of the exercise.

In spite of having intellectually grasped the concept then, I don't remember ever actually exercising free choice. For one thing, decisions rarely involved just me. There were others to consider, sometimes many many others. My choices impacted people and altered situations and I wanted to control my outcomes. Factoring and decisiveness are in opposite directions, and I couldn't have both at the same time, so I went with factoring. I thought of my style as conscientious evaluation, and the more important the choice felt to me, the more I evaluated. Admittedly, I often covered the same territory over and over before making a choice, so it was more like waffling.

Learning philosophical principles must have something in common with learning foreign languages. Lisa used to say that it takes seven distinct repetitions of a new vocabulary word before it is solidly memorized. So I might have to revisit the concept of choice another five times before it became ingrained. Focusing on decisiveness for the lunar cycle definitely counted for at least one repetition. Reviewing the definition counted for another. Such powerful words: to cut off, terminate, settle, free from doubt or wavering. I had to have this quality.

The preoccupying issue of my ex-relationship seemed to be the perfect opportunity to launch my decisiveness campaign. Larry disagreed. He said I was "forcing the flow of my experience," that what I was lacking was clarity. When I had clarity about what I wanted, then decisiveness would follow naturally. That made sense, but I was not any more successful at forcing clarity than I had been at forcing decisiveness. My effort was like hammering at a crystal ball to bring up an image.

Something Abraham said popped into my mind: "Don't give your attention to the one thing in your life that is not going well and try to fix it." Okay. There had to be evidence of decisiveness in the hundred other aspects of my life that were unfolding splendidly. Ideas started pouring in. At the ice cream counter you don't agonize over which flavor to choose, or drive away in regret, "Dang! I could have had Toasted Almond." I thought about creating a scale to measure my decisiveness, an "ice cream scale". At one end was indecisiveness ("I want some, but maybe sugar isn't such a good idea."), at the other end, straight forward preference ("Chocolate or vanilla?"), just the fun of choosing.

Scanning through my experience for areas in which I felt successful, I looked for evidence of easy "ice cream" decisions. In my career, I came up with college matches for kids almost effortlessly. I got people cycling through my schedule effectively and efficiently. In my friendships I did not hesitate to choose a walk over a movie. Exercise: a class at the gym? Yes. Shopping: what did I want for dinner? I knew exactly what I wanted—and I liked finding it on sale. Preferences came tumbling out. I started thinking with pleasure of all manner of things that appealed to me. Walking on the beach, cross-country skiing, snorkeling in warm water, laughing with friends, maternal pride, petting Casper, planning a trip, watching a movie, sitting in my garden.

A wave of pleasure followed that stream of thoughts. The delight of witnessing Law of Attraction in action. What was it that I had been thinking about? I considered retracing the thought sequence that had led me to that excellent space, but I was more inclined to just move ahead on the wave of expansiveness. Did that count as decision?

⊰ 37 ⊱

Accountability

Decisiveness was an expectation back at Fort Apache. That was an environment of authenticity and accountability. I remember a moment of revelation when Weez lit into me for standing her up one afternoon. When I protested that I had not thought of it as a commitment, she retorted, "I expect you to say what you mean, not what you think I want to hear. What you said was 'Sure,' what you meant was 'No.'" A string of broken commitments from my childhood came bubbling up to my recollection. For the first time—consciously, at least—I recognized my suppressed disappointment at being told, "That would be nice," in response to my request to go to the park. Now I got what they had meant.

Ree surprised me in a similar way back then. I knew right away that she was highly intuitive, and she recognized in me some kindred spirit, but was critical of my apparent passivity. In the course of clarifying our friendship, Ree accused me of withholding my true nature. I admitted that it had been my goal to interact with her when I was at my best. Ree responded that she was unwilling to have our friendship be on those terms. We had both read Shirley MacLaine's *Out on a Limb* and were expecting special messengers to show up in our lives. Ree was convinced that I had something important to teach her, which could only happen if I expressed it from my whole truth. Intrigued, I agreed, sensing that it would be an opening for both of us. So we embarked on a friendship of full disclosure with the intention (at first unstated, then later explicit) of becoming enlightened beings.

⚜ **38** ⚜

Enlightenment and Ree

Ree and I were always collecting snippets of spiritual philosophy to weave into our evolving understanding of the big picture. We picked up whatever we could find that might expand our understanding of the meaning of life. Of course we knew that it was not about the destination; every source we came across agreed that enlightenment was about the journey. Agreed. As soon as we had the thing figured out, we were planning to make it all about the journey. Until then, we would read books, listen to CDs, watch videos, and follow guided meditations.

Of the many guided meditations Ree and I engaged in, none came close to Subi's. Her meditations were always extraordinary, probably because she was. Subi is one of those wise people who has been on a path of enlightenment herself, trying to make sense of the loss of her daughter. As opposed to becoming bitter from grief, she turned into an open-hearted being that everyone loves.

In the days leading up to one of Subi's meditations, my excitement mounted as I imagined that it would be the one that would "do it," get me permanently into the magical space I craved. Eager for the event, I carefully formulated and stated my intentions. Ree and I would drive over to Subi's space together to share in each other's giddy anticipation. We expected something wonderful, and we were never disappointed. Each meditation took us to a new place of awareness, or felt like a profound respite for the soul, or something; no two were ever the same. Whatever it was, the magic seemed to last for weeks.

As with meditations, there were particular books that especially affected me. Deepak Chopra's, *Seven Spiritual Laws of Success* had that kind of impact on my world. I spent countless happy hours creating visions of the lifestyle I wanted, inspired by his phrase "Pure Potential."

An early source of inspiration was Shakti Gawain's video, *Creative Visualization*. One of my favorite processes from it invites you to create a mental image of whatever you desire your life to be, then picture enclosing it in a big pink bubble. Finally, you picture releasing the bubble and watching it float away from you. Granted, most of the people I described the process to failed to resonate with the pink bubble imagery, but I loved it, and even went so far as to try it with real soap bubbles.

Whenever Ree and I got together, we exchanged the new ideas we had come across in the interim. As we walked, we tried to weave the new insights into our expanding philosophy. Gray used to tease Ree about having a "religion of the month" approach. Immune to skepticism, we continued sifting through our experiences, looking for snippets relevant to our quest for enlightenment, amassing promising bits of imagery along our perceived trail "up the mountain." That expression came from a favorite joke— practically a signature joke for Ree and me—although nobody else seemed to find it funny:

> *A young man was intent on discovering the meaning of life. He questioned anyone he thought might have words of wisdom for him.*

The young man heard that there was a guru living in a remote ashram who might have the answer to his question.

So the young man set off to find the guru. When he arrived at the ashram, the young man was told that, indeed, a wise one did live there, but he lived in seclusion and came out only once every few years. Perhaps, on that rare occasion, he would oblige the young man with the answer he sought. And so the man waited patiently, living in the ashram for three years. At last the guru came out from his isolation and spoke to the man. "You are a patient man. Clearly, you have come with a question. I will answer it if I am able." Eagerly, the man asked, "What is the meaning of life?" The guru replied, "I do not know. But there is one who knows—a very wise hermit who lives in the forest on the far side of the plains."

So the man set off to cross the vast plains. Never losing sight of his objective, he journeyed for three years until he reached the forest in which the hermit lived. Realizing that the hermit was unused to company, the man waited patiently at a distance, for the hermit to become accustomed to him. Three years passed and then one day the hermit spoke, "You are a persistent man. Clearly, you have come with a question. Perhaps I have the answer to it." And so the man asked his question, "What is the meaning of life?" The hermit replied, "I do not know. But there is one who knows—an enlightened one who lives at the top of the highest mountain."

So the man set off for the mountains. Never losing sight of his objective, he climbed for three years until he reached the summit of the highest mountain. There he found the tent of the enlightened one. Cautiously, the man entered and found the enlightened one sitting in meditation, gazing into the flame of a candle. Weary from his journey, the man sat and waited for the enlightened one to address him. Without taking his eyes off the candle flame, the enlightened one spoke, "Clearly, you have come with a question. Make it known to me and I will answer it." Trembling with excitement, the man asked his question, "What is the meaning of life?" The enlightened one continued to stare into the candle flame and said, "The meaning of life is in the candle." Appalled at this ridiculous answer, the man blurted out, "No, it's not!" The enlightened one was jolted out of his meditation, "It's not!?"

It makes me laugh every time I hear it. Both Ree and I periodically proclaim, "The meaning of life is in . . . (this ice cream)."

⚜ 39 ⚜

Kripalu

Along my path to enlightenment, I found the Kripalu Center for Yoga and Health. It took me a while to recall what prompted my first visit to Kripalu. I learned about the center at a Divine Unity gathering, a weekend consisting mostly of guided meditation. Although the details of that event were not all that memorable, arriving at Kripalu for the first time was.

Ree and I had driven up to Massachusetts together. During the drive we had speculated about what the gathering would be like, and what we hoped to get out of the weekend. We were goofing off, listening to a Wayne Dyer CD and solemnly chanting "Ommmm" at each other. It was after dark when we entered the picturesque little town nearest to our destination. We pulled over and read the last few lines of our directions under a Victorian globe street lamp. Then we drove the short remaining distance with only our car's headlights cutting through the pitch dark. When we came to the sign marking the entrance to the Kripalu grounds, the energy seemed to surge. As we drove through the corridor of enormous evergreens at the entrance, Ree and I whirled to face one another in our excitement. Simultaneously we exclaimed, "Did you feel that!?" It was like some force field from Star Trek, a wondrous skin-tingling frisson of energy. We parked and entered the building quietly. At the reception desk there was a note with our names written on it directing us to our room. We were to check in the following morning.

We woke before dawn and quietly made our way down to sunrise yoga. Then we checked in and headed for breakfast. Even if the receptionist had not cautioned us, the sign-board at the entrance to the cafeteria made it abundantly clear that breakfast at Kripalu was to be a silent affair, a time to reflect and be mindful, free of perfunctory or heart-felt salutations. Ree and I took trays and worked our way down the line, piling our plates with items such as scrambled tofu, oatmeal and chopped fruit, steamed kale, fresh whole grain bread, and homemade yogurt. We sat by ourselves at a table next to a window with a view of the hill behind the center. I knew better than to make eye contact with Ree; situations like that compel her to silly antics. When I finally did glance at her, sure enough, she gave me "the look." I let out a stifled chuckle, whereupon she donned a severe expression, raised an eyebrow, and whispered a mock reprimand, "Silence!", making it impossible for me to maintain my composure. Rather than risk blowing more tea out my nasal passages, I signaled Ree to take her tray and follow me outside. We would finish our meal in the morning sun facing the lake, in the company of the other mischief-makers and those who preferred to assert themselves verbally, regardless of the hour.

Following the afternoon session of the event we were attending, Ree and I explored the grounds. We hiked up the trails through the woods and down to the lake building up an appetite for dinner. We were planning to do a drumming activity before dinner and to try out the renowned saltwater jacuzzi afterwards. Neither of us had expected such an amazing offering of culinary delights, almost entirely vegetarian, macrobiotic, or vegan. It was hard not to overdo it; we did not succeed. After dinner, we staggered down to the women's suite, stashed our clothes in one of the open bins, showered, and wearing towels, crossed the hall to the jacuzzi room. Hanging our towels on the hooks by the door, we peered through the dense fog, trying to see the steps leading down into the water. A delicate breeze from the open window over the jacuzzi swirled the rising steam. Ree and I could just make out some figures partially submerged on the other side, naked breasts bobbing in the warm bubbling water. Through the steam, a sultry voice greeted us, "Welcome to Venus."

Ree and I tried to have one weekend of R & R every season after that first visit. We got a lot out of those "R's", especially renewal. The magic seemed to sustain us until the next visit. The more time we spent there, the more exploring we did, and the more delightful aspects we discovered about the facility. It was Subi who had indirectly brought Kripalu into our lives. She had been all over seeking sources of inspiration for enlightenment. On one of her adventures in Sedona, she and Ree's Uncle, Bill had been involved in constructing labyrinths. They came back raving, and in the ensuing conversation, they asked if we had visited the labyrinth at Kripalu. That became the priority for our next visit. Any excuse for being outdoors and walking suited me, and I was intrigued by Subi's and Bill's descriptions of how inspirational the experience could be.

Unlike navigating a maze, traveling the path of a labyrinth is not dependent on logic. Your route is pre-determined; it leads in to the center, and then back out. You can maintain your introspective focus as you walk along, without any risk of losing your way. I was fascinated by my reaction to the journey. At times I was sure a turn would open to the center; instead, the path led back to the periphery. My mood dropped from eagerness to disappointment in a single step, kind of like life. At last, the opening came; I had arrived at the center. What the . . . ! A dinky Buddha statue? That was not the meaning of life! Far from enlightened, I felt petty. I had hoped for something more . . . profound. I felt the gears grinding in my mind. I knew I had to shift my focus about the experience, or I would forfeit the high I had gotten to in my anticipation of arriving there. How else could I hold it? I supposed the cheesy Buddha statue did have comic potential. That thought was all it took. I felt the emotional ease from just that little sprinkling of amusement. I made my affirmations and turned to go back just as Ree arrived at the center. She took one look at the mini shrine and erupted in laughter. I made my way back to the entrance in high humor, full of appreciation for my life.

One time Ree and Gray and their kids came to hang with us at Hopewell. The guys were in the living room with the kids, so Ree and I went to the kitchen to reminisce about our recent trip to Kripalu. I placed an unopened half gallon of Turkey Hill Peanut Butter Ripple ice cream on the counter between the two of us, and got out two iced tea spoons. Ree and I set to the task of de-veining the ribbons of peanut butter from the vanilla matrix. Some time passed; Ree and I were engrossed in our task when Seth happened by. Witnessing the results of our strip-mining zeal, he proclaimed that we looked anything but enlightened.

During our time at Kripalu, Ree and I talked about how much fun it would be to share the experience with Weez. Eventually, we persuaded her to make the quarterly pilgrimage with us. Despite her reservations about watching her closest friends diving into the deep end of all that spiritual stuff, Weez was a good sport about the trip, and she agreed to join us in all the activities we put on her "Must Do" list: yoga, vegan meals, drumming & dancing, floating in the jacuzzi, hiking down to the lake, and walking the labyrinth. In her own explorations (while Ree and I were off chanting or something), Weez found the cafe, bought a tennis outfit at the gift shop, and booked a massage. After lunch, just as we all were about to walk down to the labyrinth together, Weez's cell phone rang. She had been waiting for an important call, and wanted to take it. So Ree and I decided to go on ahead, and wait for her at the labyrinth. Weez nodded her consent, already engaged in her phone conversation.

From the open field below, we could see that Weez had not started down. The last time we had been there, it had been cold, and the cherry trees that formed an avenue leading up to the arch by the labyrinth entrance were bare. Ree and I had had to bundle up against the bracing wind. Weez would get to see it at its peak. The cherry trees were in full pink splendor, and the bright sun was warm on us and on the newly mown grass along the path. I stepped out of my sandals to feel it. When we came to the arch, the labyrinth looked so enticing we just couldn't wait for Weez. Besides, the walk was meant to be undertaken as a solo process. Ree entered first, and I waited a while, forming my intentions. Then I began my slow, mindful journey to the center, focusing on each step. A good while later, Ree passed me on her return, lost in contemplation. I spoke my affirmations at the center and was moseying back, savoring my reflections on the insights that came to me when I was distracted from my pleasant reverie by a noise. It crescendoed as I caught sight of Weez, coffee cup in one hand, cell phone to her ear, speed-walking the sacred path. Maybe humor was the meaning of life.

⊰ **40** ⊱

Practices

It wasn't just an understanding of life's grand scheme that I was interested in. My quest was finding out how to live with the most passion and vitality I could muster. After Seth and I separated, I set out to create an optimal internal environment for myself, to establish habits of well-being. I wanted to train on all three fronts, body, mind, and spirit, and I had lofty objectives for each: I would training for physical health and vigor, for a positive mental outlook, and for a greater spiritual connection with all-that-is. My aspirations were wonderful even to contemplate, and I used elements of my daily routines as anchors to those visions.

Part of the effectiveness of my rituals was due to the positive expectation I had been drilling. Each morning, I began establishing the tone of the day before I even opened my eyes. I lay in bed and made affirmations I picked up from a Louise Hay CD: "I am a deep well of love and I share it, I am joy and I feel it, I am peace and I experience it, I am infinite wisdom and I connect with it." Before any of the previous day's mental baggage floated up to my awareness, I felt for the connection with my inner guidance. Then I rose and moved with Tai Chi artistry to the mat where I stretched and did yoga.

Moving through poses, first pigeon, then thread the needle, my connection deepened. Gently twisting my spine, I felt the harmonious alignment of my whole being. Often, Casper observed my ritual from his perch in the window seat, and Buddy lay on the floor beside me, stretched out in his own version of yoga. A wave of amusement and affection would wash over me as I witnessed the natural way my companions expressed their enlightenment. I felt the need to be pro-active in mine, and reached for the laminated card Ree made for me. At the top of the card was a picture of rocks in a clear streambed; below was a statement I found moving: "I control my thoughts to make my mind purposeful and positive."

Napoleon Hill's words, "Thoughts are things," had been germinating in my mind for many years. I carefully tended the soil around them, sensing that they tied in to the ideas that filtered into my emerging philosophy. I kept coming across assertions that we could create anything we could conceive. Moreover, we were actually doing just that—albeit unconsciously. Abraham referred to it as "creating by default." I believed it could be accomplished intentionally, but I had yet to do it consistently.

Deliberate creation probably followed non-attachment. There were apparent philosophical catches throughout spiritual philosophy. In order to posses something, you had to release it. In order to feel assured in spirit, you had to have faith in it. Instead of grappling with it conceptually, I made faith a practice. I affirmed my way to believing I would prevail. I acted on the wisdom that living life by design would come through mindfulness, and made a concerted effort to focus on the details of certain actions. Walking, breathing, doing dishes, became ceremonies of awareness.

In the beginning, when I was emotionally fragile, I went to the gym to avoid being alone in an empty house. Activity filled a void. Gradually, I came to appreciate the many ways in which the whole exercise experience launched me into a powerful space. In the intense focus of an activity, my mental chatter receded. The music seemed to vibrate through me, and I lost track of time. Sometimes I indulged myself with a bubble massage by floating in the jacuzzi afterwards. When I walked out to my car feeling, I felt carefree and restored to my inherent well-being.

Eating became a mindful activity, too. I began noting my mood when I felt inclined to eat. In the beginning, I had used "sugar therapy" to compensate for stress. That happened less and less as I became attentive to my motivation to eat. It wasn't all about salad. Once I was struck with an intense craving for dark chocolate mini peanut butter cups from Trader Joe's. No way I was going to deny an urge that strong, besides that store always had good energy for me. It took a lot of control not to rip open the container before I made it through the register line. I waited until I cleared the exit before fumbling through the shopping bag. I seized the container and tore off the plastic seal. Isolating my first cup, I peeled back the wrapper and sank my teeth through the dark chocolate top, through the core, and through to the bottom. The dark chocolate at the bottom of the cup was disproportionately thick. Encountering the relative magnitude of that layer sent a paroxysm of sublime emotion rippling through the pleasure center of my brain.

Trader Joe's mini peanut butter cups became my mental entry for "delicious taste." For "intoxicating fragrance," it was honeysuckle on a summer breeze; For "stirring scene," the sun setting on snow-covered mountains; For "happy sound," the boys' laughter; For "wonderful touch," stroking the fur under Casper's chin. When he slept in the corner next to my pillow, I got to experience that one physically before I fell asleep. I liked to go through my list of delightful sensations as I drifted off each night. It was part of the momentum I set in motion for the next morning.

⪪ 41 ⪫

Dreams

CONSTRUCTION MATERIALS

In the course of my mindfulness campaign, I began recalling my dreams from the previous night. It was not due to a streak of good fortune or happenstance; I had been purposeful in setting the stage for recollection. For starters, I set the intention to remember them before I fell asleep. Then I got into the habit of waking slowly, keeping my eyes closed for a few seconds, and jotting down notes first thing when I woke up.

When I was younger, I was really interested in dream analysis. Dreams no longer seemed like mystical portals to me, just easy ways to get insight into my subconscious. I was really only interested in how I felt during a dream or when I thought about it afterwards. Dreams were either pleasant, or they were disconcerting. I liked identifying the construction materials that went into them, recognizing the source of the elements that I wove together into the dreamscape.

In a recent dream, I was walking around a table at which several people I was counseling were seated. They were doing some arts-and-crafts project that involved mixing food color into containers of modeling compound. Although

I had given precise instructions for one particular step, I turned my attention to one woman just in time to watch her squirt a stream of red dye into her container, rather than meter out just one drop. In a flash, I saw that several of the others were poised to do as she had done with their tiny squeeze bottles, and blurted out, "Just a drop! That's enough to feed an army."

Outside my dream, Buddy caused a floorboard to creak as he exited the room. The sound accelerated me through the transition from dream state to waking, and I missed any chance for slowly dawning insight.

The dream did not come with any emotional overtones that I could recall; I had felt neutral while I was dreaming and afterwards in my brief post-dream analysis. Identifying the construction materials was easy: there had been red velvet cake in the faculty lounge the day before, and someone had cautioned me to pick it up with a napkin lest the food dye stain my fingers. And Ree had texted me about Daniel's latest escapades in China. He had just seen the Terra Cotta Army. Random snippets. An infinite array of dreams could have been constructed using those two elements. In a different arrangement, I might have shared Red Zinger tea with pandas, or sliced cherry pie with chopsticks.

BIRD-CREATURES

Another time, I dreamed I was standing with Jordan, on a ledge out in the ocean. No worries. There was a crowd of others with us, waiting. The medium shifted to air. From above, a huge flock of strange tiny bird-like creatures approached, then flew straight through the crowd. Someone signaled that we each should try to catch one. There was a titter of excitement and a flurry of motion as the bird-creatures streaked by us. Some of the younger kids jumped up to snag bird-creatures coursing above them. On closer inspection, the bird-creatures were made of wood, delicately carved and painted. Nonetheless, they were sentient. One by one those who had secured bird-creatures were lifted off like seeds of dandelion fluff into the air current. The crowd was thinning rapidly as more and more were streaming up and away. I watched one kid make slow uncoordinated movements. The bird-creature he tried for flew off. My thoughts came in a cluster. He's not really trying; he's counting on someone else to procure a bird-creature for him, but that wouldn't happen because soon, everyone else would be carried away. Did he not expect to catch one? And would that negative expectation ensure his failure? I wondered what would happen to him, but was distracted by my own lift-off. The bird-creature I held was warm and still in my grasp. I was pondering its lack of struggle when I noticed that the boy—the one I had feared might be left behind—was floating with the others in the air stream. The flaw turned out to be my own negative expectation that his defeatist attitude would doom him. I was relieved that he had somehow succeeded, but confused about how it had all worked out. Had there been a slow bird-creature to match his effort? I didn't finish that thought either, as I was plunked down somewhere along a dirt road beside a snow-covered fallow field. As I was picking myself up and getting ready to move on, Jordan was deposited nearby in the field. We must have ridden on similar air currents. Somehow I knew that we were the only ones there; the others were in a different reality. Jordan joined me and we set off walking along the road toward the red-orange horizon. We chatted about our flight as the gloaming light faded.

Casper kneaded my shoulder, rousing me just in time to see the gorgeous red dawn. The light morphed to yellow-orange within minutes. The words "There's a logic to optimism," were still clear in my mind, as if I had heard them spoken aloud. I closed my eyes and lay still for a moment, recollecting the dream: overarching well-being, things working out despite apparent obstacles, everyone benefitting, being included in the moving on, but judgement and doubt on my part. I changed my focus: even when I don't expect things to work out, they work out. Much better. I like thinking that things work out for everybody, no exceptions. I like that there are similarities, overlaps, common experiences. But what to make of the fallow field, with nothing but corn stalk stubble, covered with snow in the fading light? Re-focus: that dream construction element had come from my recent recollection of a delightful meadow in wintertime. I had just remembered a wonderful late afternoon of cross-country skiing. In the fading light of that beautiful sunset, there had been excitement; we had hurried to cross the meadow before dark. Walking and talking with Jordan symbolized intellectual stimulation, and companionship. The flying theme, getting swept up and carried forward—by birds, no less!—gave a sense of something uplifting and instinctual. Even my critique of my own faulty thinking indicated that I was reconsidering the way I looked at the big picture. I took it as evidence of my evolution.

DRIVING ON TWO WHEELS

My dreams were always illuminating, even when they were not cheery. In one curious dream, I was driving an older model white four-door sedan on a highway somewhere. Seth and Jesse were in the back seat. Very slowly, I felt the car begin to roll sideways until it was riding only on the two driver side tires. I recognized that I was choosing not to panic, instead just staying focused on my mental image of the tires' surfaces spreading out under the load where they contacted the road, and picturing the expanded region advancing in steady rotation as the tires rolled along.

I realized we were accelerating toward a more developed area. That puzzled me because I was not stepping on the gas, and the road was level. Nonetheless we were gaining momentum, but I deliberately kept calm. As long as I could maintain the car on its side, not flipped completely over, I knew somehow I could get it to roll back down right; I just needed time to get the feel of it on its side. I recognized that my attitude was critical to succeeding. I was choosing not to let panicky thinking derail my deliberate observation. I would attentively ride it out and find a successful conclusion. But Seth was panicked and was yelling directions and criticism at me from the back seat. That distracted me, and I started to focus on the fact that we were accelerating toward something like a toll plaza, and that cars were traversing our lane ahead. Seth kept barking instructions at me, but I could not process them and maintain the focus that was critical to our precarious balance. I understood that my focused attention was somehow keeping us from tipping. Seth was insisting that I had to do something about the cruise control setting, but I didn't want to take my eyes off the road for even a second to figure out what he was insisting on. He got more and more demanding. Finally, I diverted some of my focus and spoke, "I don't know what you mean; you'll have to explain it better." We were about to get into the congested area, and I began to feel anxious about not actually knowing how it was that I was controlling the car, and therefore unsure how I could continue to do so. The dream ended there.

The construction materials were obvious to me. The day before, I had come across a Mensa Mind Bender and it had bent my mind. I felt myself shift from excitement about the mental exercise, to frustration at not grasping it. Also, while I was driving around, I was listening to an Abraham-Hicks download. My I-pod started playing at a crazy speed like a 45 record playing on 78. Abraham often said, "When you're out of control, you might as well ride it out." When I reflected on the dream, although I was not crazy about getting taken off my game, I loved how I had kept my focus and tried not let any outside influence derail me.

WANTING TO FLY

Sometimes I got so absorbed in the feeling of my dreams that I didn't remember to register the dream's more concrete elements. That happened when I dreamed I was at a spacious lodge in the Canadian Rockies. Some acquaintances and I were there for some sort of convention. The next scheduled conference event was to take place a short distance away, across a lake from the lodge where we were staying. A fellow attendee and I were walking in the parking lot to get in a car and drive across the bridge to the venue. The air was cool and refreshing, and I kept taking long, deep, deliberate breaths. The colors were vibrant on the slopes of the majestic mountains all around. Gray granite, white snow, emerald evergreens. Directly ahead of us, a tiny plane took off from a single strip runway at the side of the lodge; it rose into the brilliant sky. I recognized Ree as the pilot. Enthusiasm over the idea of flying flooded through me, but I couldn't think of a way to contact Ree and ask her to circle back and pick me up. Even though I was drinking in the beauty of my surroundings and in no hurry to get anywhere, I knew that driving would just seem pathetically slow after having recognized such a powerful preference for flying. I wanted the rush of height and speed.

I woke feeling elated, and my excitement continued as I realized that it was my wanting that had felt exhilarating. I was thrilled that the act of desiring had been the cause for my happiness. The construction materials were easy to recognize. The tiny plane idea came from a recent counseling business trip in which I had flown in a private jet to the Finger Lakes to check out a college. When I returned, I told Weez and Ree how easy it had been, and that we should go off on an impulse excursion somewhere. The Canada element came from having come across an old postcard of Banff while cleaning out the attic. I thought it would make a fun excursion. The lodge became a convention center.

Since that dream occurred on a Saturday morning, I did not trouble to rouse myself, and slipped back down under for more. When I surfaced later, I almost caught another dream. But Casper was not patient enough to wait for the enlightened insight that often comes in the transition to full awareness. He announced, "Breakfast" with conviction. Walking downstairs, I started to give my dream a Psych 101 level analysis. By the time I had fed the cat and walked Buddy, I had completely forgotten it. No big deal, I remembered the important part: I had enjoyed it.

⪥ **42** ⪤

Dating

It felt good to think of myself as the architect of my life. I liked being explicit about what I wanted for and from myself. I had been filling journals with my reflections and prioritizing my desires and values. Even though I was certain I was the source of my own happiness, I was resisting my friends' and co-workers' invitations to set up dates for me. I wanted to be even more solid in my non-dependence. But I knew the time would come when I would be drawn to start dating. I had adopted Abraham's philosophy regarding relationships, that the greatest gift that you can give a person you care about is "I'm not looking to you for my happiness." Meanwhile, I would look for examples of what I did like in other couples.

I remembered a conversation in which some phrase had prompted Ree and Gray to break into a musical number from "South Pacific," laughing through their vocal harmony, filling in one another's missed lyrics. I made a mental note to move "playful" to the top of my list of desirable attributes.

⊰ **43** ⊱

Valentine's Day

One beautiful morning I was drifting just below the surface of self-awareness. I lay still, trying to prolong the transition before the download of my day's agenda flooded in. For a few moments I back-paddled to catch the remnants of my dream, but it dissolved before I could reconstruct it.

Apricot light flickered on the window sill. Casper was at his usual post in the window seat, perfectly aligned with the beam of sunlight that filtered through the branches of the cherry tree outside. He rose with a stretch that rippled into a taut bow, then settled back into his spot. Usually, he sensed my awakening, but that morning he was not insisting on breakfast. I was glad for the rare treat of lying in bed after sunrise. It took me a while to find the title of the tune that had been playing in my mind, and when I did, it made me smile. "If I Had Words (to make a day for you)." I took a deep breath, and released it slowly. Then I remembered what day it was.

People in secure relationships are quick to say that Valentine's Day is no big deal. I used to feel that way. So it came as a surprise to learn how big a deal it seemed in my newly-single state. My concerns were largely based in appearances. Anticipating my associates' reports on their romantic escapades, I did not want to have to say I had watched a movie by myself, and have them speculate about my isolation. If I did not clean up my yucky focus, I was likely to find myself an actual victim of pity—my own self-pity.

In the past, I had always liked Valentine's Day; I had thought of it as a celebration of love. Having switched sides of the couples/singles line, the holiday now seemed little more than an occasion for a commitment check up, with two possibilities: you were moving toward or moving away from commitment. On the one side, you could count on getting a card and flowers or dinner, maybe both, and for courting couples, sex. On the side where I was, . . . zip. The best I could count on was my annual Valentine's card from "The Cat". (Ree was good with the card thing.) I was rooted in the zone of romantic fantasizing, and I was bummed about it. Fortunately, I did not have to stay in that space; I could get myself redirected and ease my way to a better-feeling mindset. I knew how to do that.

I started by thinking about how I wanted to feel—not what I wanted to have. I was not going to have a Valentine's date or card or flowers. Over those specifics, I had no control, but over my feelings, I reigned sovereign. I needed something to reinforce the burgeoning recognition that the solution to my relationship woes was being responsible for my own happiness. Remembering that was the first thread of the sturdy rope I was going to braid.

My formula for feeling good had always included nature and companionship. Easy enough. I could enjoy walking along the canal where there was freshly fallen snow. I could even cross-country ski there. Activity would be a plus. I was reluctant to invite anyone to join me lest it pull them away from some Valentine's day plans. Just as I was thinking that, Ree called. I had not factored in her complete confidence in the stability of her relationship with Gray. I heard her call out to him, did he mind . . . ? followed by her assurance that he was fine skipping the compulsory Valentine's ceremonies. Ree said she would love to have an outing with me. I had a date!

I have always had a thing for snow; just thinking about it gives me a thrill. I had worked up a passion for skiing before I had ever experienced it, and when I did, it exceeded my expectations. Being in any kind of nature raises my energy, but mountains and water make my spirits soar. Likewise, taking a walk in any weather is great, but in winter it is especially invigorating. Most exhilarating of all is gliding silently on skis through the crisp air.

Ree proposed we go cross-country skiing through the open fields of the nature preserve near her. She and I liked to visit "the meadow" at least once a season. We had seen the fields cycle from a wintery taupe when they were fallow, to a lime green as the sprouts broke through in spring. Various shades of green emerged as the crops grew lush and became decorated with tiny wildflowers, and finally, when the grasses rose to a five foot tall sea, the field waved from green to gold and then to brown again. On that Valentine's day, it was white.

In addition to open fields, the preserve has woods and trails that wind down to a babbling creek. Some sections are quite steep and tricky to run down. On one of my favorite parts of the path through the meadow there is an awkwardly banked stretch that takes a sharp bend out of sight. The footing there is tricky, in part because of deeply etched channels carved by rivulets of the rainwater that gush through the natural trough of the path during heavy downpours. Also, the grass on that stretch is irregularly trodden and can be slick. All the aforementioned complexities contribute to the rush you get, running down it at breakneck speed. You have to flail your arms and brake with rapid tiny steps to negotiate the sharp turn at the bottom, as the momentum from accelerating down the straight part and the pitch at the start of the turn would otherwise force you to fly straight ahead and over the edge of the path. I always look down to watch my footing when I go for it. Once, just as I hit the turn, I encountered a fellow nature-lover coming from the other side. The startle was all it took to break my concentration, and I barreled tangentially off the turn and over the bank below. The innocent hiker watched in stupefied horror as I brushed past him, screaming, "Aaaaaaaaa . . ." in my precarious flight.

It was late in the afternoon when I got my stuff together and met Ree. We knew we would have to get a move on to catch the remaining daylight. The sun was already setting and there were beautiful streaks of salmon-gold reflecting off of the high clouds. The meadow would have been noisy with chirping birds and buzzing insects in August, but at twilight in February, it was magically still. We shuffled to the top of the first steep hill and sort of dared one another to take it straight down—always tricky in unpacked snow because it was easy to catch a tip and go tumbling. But the risk added to the excitement. I heard Ree shriek off to my side, but I didn't dare take my eyes off my ski tips, and plowed on, gathering momentum. Ree's shriek turned to laughter and receded, so I knew she had taken a nosedive. Within minutes she caught up, and we continued together, bounding up the next hill. As we rounded the turn at the top, we could see the last amber glow of the sun and the already darkening sky opposite. We decided not to complete the circuit lest we run out of light in time to do it safely, so we turned around and headed back. The cold air and exercise had given me an appetite, and I knew what I was in the mood for—Mexican food.

Ree was happy with my choice, and we drove to Baja Fresh. That was before it closed down. I have been in a kind of mourning ever since. What Baja Fresh lacked in ambience, it more than made up for in taste. That night was one of many fond memories there. I ordered my usual, a bean and cheese burrito bursting at the seams with pico de gallo, guacamole, mango salsa, and cilantro. Ree and I fell into our routine; she went for the water and lime while I hoarded supplies from the condiment bar. We sat in our favorite booth, close to the condiment bar, and fell into an animated review of what a blast skiing across the meadow had been. We talked and crunched nachos. I was saying, "This has been the perfect Valentine's day," when my phone rang. The call was from my most recent match.com wink, inviting me to meet him at a nearby book store. He got extra points for his choice of venue. I was as excited about the magical timing of his invitation as I was about the idea of our meeting for the first time.

When I dropped Ree off at her house, I ran in and brushed my teeth; that was it for my date preparation. I drove off feeling gorgeous and confident, glad that he was going to meet me as I was, free of make-up, with hat-hair, dressed in my cross-country ski outfit. It was easy to spot him; he was strikingly handsome and conspicuously sexy. He made it obvious that my assessment was reciprocated. We hit it off instantly, and the conversation was engaging, easy, and intimate. Our spontaneous meeting over tea at a book store was incredibly romantic. I could not have designed a more delightful Valentine's Day.

⊰ **44** ⊱

Spring Break

Dating turned out to be especially enjoyable when I stayed attuned to my authentic emotions, and kept my focus positive. I was not looking for my dates to fill an emotional void; I was discovering common ground and sharing interesting activities with them. It was refreshing to take each occasion as a celebration of me, my confidence, and expanding clarity.

Part of living mindfully meant balancing my social time with alone time, and making the most of unclaimed time. When Spring Break rolled around, several options competed for my precious vacation days. There were projects around the house on my "As Soon As I Have Time" list, and I was looking forward to staying home. But as I was drifting off to sleep one night, remembering how much fun it had been listening to the more exotic destinations of my co-workers, I amended my list to include travel—preferably to someplace warm. The next day, a former colleague called and invited me to join her in Santa Fe for the break, enticing me with descriptions of the views of mountains from her porch. I did not waffle; I booked a flight that evening.

Jennifer's description did not do justice to the splendor surrounding us in Santa Fe. One warm sunny morning we packed sunscreen and snowshoes, and drove up to a nearby mountain. At 12,000 feet we parked the car, slathered ourselves with sunscreen, strapped on our snowshoes, and strode off across the deep snow to attempt climbing the remaining 2000 feet to the summit. The mountain air and the stunning vistas gave me a high; I just could not get enough. We hiked on a path through pine forests, and then broke trail through a sea of aspens. It was an enchanted forrest; the aspen trees—which extended as far as I could see—seemed to emanate a palpable energy. I felt compelled to embrace one. Jennifer watched in amusement at first, then she, too, succumbed to the magic and hugged one. I started to feel lightheaded from the altitude, but decided to push on. My mind translated, "This is a peak moment," and I laughed at the pun. In that rush of happiness, I felt resilient and powerful—a wonderful combination.

We sat at the top and rested before heading back down, then drove home in quasi silence, each marinating in our own exercise euphoria. That afternoon, we sat out by the pool, and soaked up the warm sun. The finishing touch for the day was a memorable meal of al dente linguini and fragrant burgundy. We ate outside sipping and twirling, watching the magenta sunset across the mountains. As the light faded, and the rose spectrum blended into the turquoise sky along the horizon, the first stars began to twinkle overhead.

⊰ 45 ⊱

Morning Bike Ride

When I was in alignment with my love for life, everyday experiences like my morning bike ride to work could put me in a state of almost euphoric well-being. One splendid morning, the mist was still rising off the lawns when I set out. I could tell that it was going to get hot later on, but right then there was a pleasant breeze. There were not yet many cars on the road, so it was quiet enough to hear birds all around. I pedaled along easily and caught the first hint of a fragrance. Within seconds it grew intense then faded like an olfactory Doppler wave. As the delicious smell peaked, I saw honeysuckle winding through the shrubbery on a wooded lot.

An elderly gentleman was collecting his morning paper. I greeted him enthusiastically with, "Have a good day!" He replied, "I just did," and we both laughed. Then I pedaled by a garden that took my breath away. It was dazzling with color and variety. A woman was meticulously weeding her horticultural masterpiece. I complimented her, "Your garden is a pure delight," and felt the pride in her reply, "I'm so glad you appreciate it." I rounded a bend and encountered a woman walking an ancient Beagle. I had seen this same pair out walking as I drove to work a year ago. Back then, when I looked at the geriatric dog, creeping along on his naturally stubby legs, I figured he had maybe two weeks to live. Yet there they were a year later, the old dog inching his way along, his owner lovingly encouraging him every inch of the way. I stopped my bike to let them pass slowly in the crosswalk. The woman smiled at me warmly. Her love for the dog was palpable; it made my heart swell. I felt so in tune with the people I encountered that I had the sense I was experiencing their feelings empathetically. When I rode up to the crossing guard I felt her rush of pleasure as kids streamed by her on their bikes.

I arrived at work so emotionally high that I induced a resonant enthusiasm in my co-workers when I related my experiences to them. I was delighted to find that such a powerful sense of connection and love had come from my interaction with relative strangers. I realized I could access those treasured emotions any time I tuned myself to them.

⇥ **46** ⇤

Culmination

More and more I was getting evidence that the life I wanted to design was being revealed all around me. It seemed to culminate in one magical evening. I joined Ree and Gray and their family and friends to watch Daniel play the lead in his high school musical, "Les Misérables." I had seen the play on Broadway years before, and had found it moving, but I found Daniel's production to be a far more stirring experience. It was amazing to see one of "our" kids so poised and powerful, clearly having come into his own. I was flooded with emotion. I sat next to Daniel's grandmother, Pam. At one point, without taking her eyes off the stage, she slipped me a handkerchief. Lisa was there, too, along with Subi, and Weez, and Larry. Susan was on stage, part of the performance. Her enchanting soprano voice seemed to vibrate straight into me. It was the intensity of the whole experience that struck me, the presence of the elements I had included in my description of perfect love: keen interest, piqued anticipation, common emotional experience, even physical arousal from the music and the scene, with the added connection of shared history. I felt choked up with tender sentiment, engulfed by a love I had not even consciously sought. My world changed that evening, and I moved into a new dimension of appreciation.

⊰ **47** ⊱

Self-Awareness

When I zoomed out, I discovered a perspective from which my story seemed uncomplicated—even positive. With an awareness akin to subliminal recognition, somehow natural yet unfamiliar, I saw myself as a small yet integral part of something immense. What had seemed like randomness in my story seemed logically ordered from there. I instinctively knew that all the events of my life had culminated in that understanding.

In a download of insight, I got that the key to my well-being lay in self-awareness. It was that simple and that brilliant. I was infused with peace knowing that things were fine from my broader perspective, and I wanted more than anything else to stay connected with that expanded me. It had been wonderful seeing things in that light, and I sensed that I had only tapped the surface. From there, the events of my life, that I had been holding as problems, were just scenes along an ongoing journey. Beyond hope or possibility, I knew that from that point on I would move forward into new chapters, and that my happiness would unfold before me as I moved along in harmony with myself.

My intention to maintain that connectedness kept me focused on the harmony that surrounded me, and I experienced the pieces of my world coming together in concert. Although I knew that it hadn't been that long ago, my time of intense unhappiness seemed to be in the remote past. Instead, it seemed that I had been living in a long stretch of ease. That was what I always asked the universe for, ease and flow. An eternal cycle of activity and rest, of expansion and reflection.

There was a new moon, and I knew I would soon feel the subtle stirring for some fresh awareness brewing in me. My desire for more clarity, or to refine a specific intention for positive development would wax and wane from inspiration to appreciation as I witnessed the unfolding of my new experience. I had an inkling about the source of my next wave of expansion. Of the four categories on Abraham's Guided Meditations CD, General Well-Being, Financial Abundance, Physical Well-Being, and Relationships, it was the latter I felt most drawn to listen to. Although I had listened to it many times, and had resonated with the words, a particular statement got my attention: "If you will release all concern about how others feel about you, and focus only upon how you feel about them, you will unearth your core understanding of *who-you-really-are*, and you will discover what true freedom really is."

I felt some insight working its way up to the surface as I mulled over that statement, and my eagerness made me expect that when I succeeded in peeling off that next layer, I would get to take a bold stride toward the freedom Abraham alluded to. Despite the dissatisfactory conclusion to my marriage with Seth, I felt that I had some special wisdom regarding relationships. I don't know how I knew, but I did know that my ability to love was my greatest gift. "Release all concern . . ." How do I feel about others? Tapped in to the fountainhead of love. A geyser of positive emotion. In the space of my most powerful, limitless creativity. Euphoric.

Once I started speaking words of love, I became awash with joy. The language colored my world. My perspective widened to encompass all-that-is, and I felt connected to it, a part of it. All-that-is and I were mutually in love.

⊰ **48** ⊱

Allowing

The morning was quiet and still when I emerged from sleep. Keeping my eyes closed, I hovered in the transition, wanting to draw it out as long as possible.

I began tuning in to my breathing. An image came to me of an area that extended above my head, a space my broader self occupied. I pictured my breathing as a rhythmic exchange between this broader part of me and my body, an undulating pattern of drawing the space into my body in troughs as I inhaled, and extending my tangible aspect into the space in crests as I exhaled. Then the expression "breathing through the whole body" came into my mind, evoking images of beams radiating from every surface of my physical being, through which I could breathe. Right away I felt a frisson of energy which I interpreted as confirmation that my image was consistent with that of my broader perspective. Instead of the alternating exchange I had pictured earlier, the new image was like an intuitive dance partnership. My expanded self and I were one, a spherical entity that breathed in harmony. It was as if I experienced my broader self breathing me. A wonderful lightness accompanied the inclusive perspective, and I wanted to prolong that sense of effortless blending.

Something had shifted in my overall perspective. It was a subtle shift, but I knew I was forever altered. It was as if I had thought of myself as singular prior to that experience, and afterwards, I thought of myself as plural—not split or fragmented—just no longer alone. I had experienced a blending with my higher self, and it had been sweet. I wanted more.

⤐ **49** ⤏

Communion

Before the morning was even underway I knew it would be a magical day. I went to the lake to meditate and write. Mist was rising off the water. Shards of sunlight were breaking through here and there around me, glinting off the water and beaming in flashes of intense color from the trees and sky. I took a sip of the water I had prepared the night before with slices of lime and cucumber. The delicate flavor was delicious. Silvery condensation glistened in beads around the cool bottle, and I was struck by how beautiful it looked. Magical elements were coalescing. I was having a "moment," and it just kept extending. Toasty warm face feathered by refreshing cool air. Blazing sun and billowing mist. The light was so bright that images appeared to be surrounded by haloes of complimentary colors. As though my retinal cones were burned out from staring into the sun, it was a kaleidoscope scene full of brilliant contrast.

I pictured myself with my arms positioned as if in a Hula, one extended out to the side, the other in a parallel line across my chest. Encircling me from behind, was a loving presence, a being that seemed to flow through me, yet was distinct from my form. My spirit partners' form mirrored mine, an ephemeral appendage extending alongside my outstretched arm, another appendage wrapped around my torso cradling my other arm in a nebulous embrace. Together we swayed in perfect synchronicity. I was fully aware that my physical form was standing alone and still, by the lake. At the same time, I felt intensely happy, recognizing that I had connected with some form of love, more tangible than it had ever been in my experience. My ongoing communion had begun with the who-I-really-am of my meditations.

⚔ **50** ⚔

Expansive Love

The love I had felt from my space of connection with the whole of me had been more vast than any I had felt until then. It felt as though my capacity to love had expanded.

My marvelous-magical feeling was intense for that afternoon and the following morning. It lingered pleasantly for the next few days. Off and on during that time I felt myself trying to recapture that vivid feeling—trying, but not succeeding in getting any higher on the emotional scale than hopeful.

Over the next few days, the recollection of that magical space dimmed and became like a souvenir, incapable of reviving the experience it is associated with. Intellectually, I accepted that cycling in and out of alignment was an inherent part of life's dynamic endless stream. I would always be seeking and finding joy. In my journal, I wrote: "Happiness is not a destination; it is the result of appreciation, and that can be cultivated." That was two days ago. I resisted the negative feelings that followed.

This morning I woke and felt resolve, strength, resignation, whatever. I knew I was ready to move forward, and I knew I would find relief when I did. This was a familiar place; it was the starting place. It was my in-the-moment reality, the only place I ever was. All I could start with was what was at hand, and that would be enough.

Where I was was steeped in disappointment. That very admission, and the knowledge that my intention was to become realigned, felt like positive movement. I went on: I can't believe I'm here after being so high. I'm disappointed by my disappointment. I've been dwelling on a question that I don't want an answer to: "Why doesn't it last?" and feeling resentful in my desperation to disavow my feelings.

Now I could progress. I had identified the real issue. I was the seeker in the story about the candle, and I had balked at my own proclamation: "Happiness is not a destination." I had been fervently hoping that it was, and I was heartily discouraged that I had not been able to sustain the magic I had summoned.

Now that I knew precisely what I was suffering from, I could talk myself off that ledge. It was a matter of forward focus. *That* I was good at. I began my realignment:

> I don't have to feel apprehensive about perceived setbacks because I know how to bring myself back into alignment.
>
> I like knowing that I am the creator of my circumstances.
>
> I used to think of being responsible for my circumstances as a burden; now I think of it as a privilege. I take that as evidence that my mind is opening.
>
> It feels good to accept that there will always be contrast in life.
>
> I prefer excitement to numbness.
>
> I like the idea of changing my perspective on issues, seeing where I've gotten away from my core principles.

I agree with the saying: "You are never too far along the wrong path to turn around." Picking up on my misalignment after such a long time just means that my slide back into alignment is all the more gratifying.

I am an eternally-evolving being. Change is inherent in evolution. As I change, my perspective will change, and I will have to come into alignment with that newly-expanded perspective.

There is cause for celebration in coming into alignment, and since there will always be opportunities to do so, there will always be cause for celebration.

In my alignment I am a loving, playful, enthusiastic being.

I know how to restore my natural joyous equilibrium.

I embrace life; I take it as an exciting romp.

I have arrived back in my natural domain, and I know that I will depart this blissful state again and again, only to return again and again.

I love this state because it is who I am; who I am is love.

About the Author

Lee Ann Perry has been a counselor for over twenty years. Her career has allowed her to do what she enjoys most—uplift people. She is the proud mother of two sons. A nature enthusiast, Lee loves outdoor activities: hiking, biking, cross country skiing, boating, and sitting still by the water's edge. While creating this book, she discovered her latest passion—writing.